Problems of
the United States
as World Trader
and Banker

Hal B. Lary

NATIONAL BUREAU OF ECONOMIC RESEARCH

1963

STUDIES IN INTERNATIONAL ECONOMIC RELATIONS
NUMBER 1

This study was made possible by funds granted by the Rockefeller Foundation. The Rockefeller Foundation is, however, not to be understood as approving or disapproving by virtue of its grant any of the statements made or views expressed herein.

RELATION OF THE DIRECTORS
TO THE WORK AND PUBLICATIONS
OF THE NATIONAL BUREAU OF ECONOMIC RESEARCH

1. The object of the National Bureau of Economic Research is to ascertain and to present to the public important economic facts and their interpretation in a scientific and impartial manner. The Board of Directors is charged with the responsibility of ensuring that the work of the National Bureau is carried on in strict conformity with this object.

2. To this end the Board of Directors shall appoint one or more Directors of Research.

3. The Director or Directors of Research shall submit to the members of the Board, or to its Executive Committee, for their formal adoption, all specific proposals concerning researches to be instituted.

4. No report shall be published until the Director or Directors of Research shall have submitted to the Board a summary drawing attention to the character of the data and their utilization in the report, the nature and treatment of the problems involved, the main conclusions, and such other information as in their opinion would serve to determine the suitability of the report for publication in accordance with the principles of the National Bureau.

5. A copy of any manuscript proposed for publication shall also be submitted to each member of the Board. For each manuscript to be so submitted a special committee shall be appointed by the President, or at his designation by the Executive Director, consisting of three Directors selected as nearly as may be one from each general division of the Board. The names of the special manuscript committee shall be stated to each Director when the summary and report described in paragraph (4) are sent to him. It shall be the duty of each member of the committee to read the manuscript. If each member of the special committee signifies his approval within thirty days, the manuscript may be published. If each member of the special committee has not signified his approval within thirty days of the transmittal of the report and manuscript, the Director of Research shall then notify each member of the Board, requesting approval or disapproval of publication, and thirty additional days shall be granted for this purpose. The manuscript shall then not be published unless at least a majority of the entire Board and a two-thirds majority of those members of the Board who shall have voted on the proposal within the time fixed for the receipt of votes on the publication proposed shall have approved.

6. No manuscript may be published, though approved by each member of the special committee, until forty-five days have elapsed from the transmittal of the summary and report. The interval is allowed for the receipt of any memorandum of dissent or reservation, together with a brief statement of his reasons, that any member may wish to express; and such memorandum of dissent or reservation shall be published with the manuscript if he so desires. Publication does not, however, imply that each member of the Board has read the manuscript, or that either members of the Board in general, or of the special committee, have passed upon its validity in every detail.

7. A copy of this resolution shall, unless otherwise determined by the Board, be printed in each copy of every National Bureau book.

(Resolution adopted October 25, 1926,
as revised February 6, 1933, and February 24, 1941)

Contents

*In this study, the form 1960-1961 is used to designate a period covering both the
first and second year specified; 1960-61 to designate a shorter period covering parts
of two calendar years.*

Tables

Charts

Preface

This study is an exploratory essay on problems arising out of recent changes in our international trade and payments position. It is the first report to emerge from a new program of research in this area started by the National Bureau in 1960 with the assistance of a grant from the Rockefeller Foundation. The main purpose animating this initial exercise is to identify problems and to assist in the selection of topics on which further research might usefully be undertaken by the National Bureau or others. Given, however, the current importance of these problems, the present study seeks to illuminate them by drawing upon and, within modest limits, adding to existing knowledge about our international position.

Twenty years ago, in a study of the balance of payments during the interwar period, published by the Department of Commerce in 1943 under the title *The United States in the World Economy*, I was largely concerned with the impact of this country's economic behavior and policies on other countries. From that point of view, the most striking and, in its ultimate consequences, perhaps most fateful phenomenon of that period was the contraction by more than two-thirds from 1929 to 1932 in the gross amount of dollars paid out by the United States to other countries on goods, services, and long-term investment. This was one of the external manifestations of the Great Depression—the shrinkage in our economic activity and employment and therewith in our demand for imports, the fall in commodity prices, and the cessation of our foreign investment activity. One of the principal conclusions emerging from that study was therefore "the fundamental importance of maintaining a more stable and ample flow of dollars in our transactions with other countries."

Judged by that standard, our performance in the world economy has been greatly superior since the Second World War. True, certain of our trading partners most dependent on the American market— especially Canada, the Latin American countries, and Japan—may have reason to complain about the level, regularity, or rate of growth of our demand as it affects their exports. But in our global trade and payments relations of the last several years the problem has been rather the reverse of what it had been before the last war. The flow of dollar payments to other countries has appeared all too buoyant, and the size and stability of our receipts from them have given cause for concern. Though the impact of our economic behavior and policies on other countries remains of key importance in the world economy, the United States economy is now itself more exposed than at any time in recent decades to influences from abroad and to inhibitions stemming from the prolonged weakness in its balance of payments, the cumulative reduction in its net international reserves, and the mobility of private capital.

The focus in this study is on the problems of assessing the elements of strength and weakness in our international trade and financial position and of improving adjustment processes so as to diminish the external constraint on our domestic, as well as foreign, economic policies. Attention is also given, more briefly, to the problem of making adaptations in our monetary and fiscal policies to prevent our increased international exposure from handicapping us in the pursuit of economic stability and growth. To the extent that policies are discussed, the aim is not to develop specific proposals but to indicate alternatives and to suggest some of the considerations which need to be borne in mind in weighing them.

The present essay grapples with problems which are in continuous evolution. Assessments and assumptions based on present knowledge may be swiftly proved wrong by the turn of events. Even our knowledge of the present leaves many gaps. Nowhere is this more true than in the area of cost and price comparisons between the United States and other countries, as is, I think, made clear in this report. It is startling to contrast how little is actually known on this subject with its importance to our international position and with the amount of comment and generalization about it. With the assistance of a grant from the National Science Foundation, the National Bureau has embarked on a project which, it is hoped, will provide a better basis for an appraisal of how our prices compare with those of our leading competitors. This investigation is being carried on by Irving Kravis, Robert Lipsey, and Philip Bourque.

A collateral study is being conducted by H. G. Georgiadis with a view to seeing what can be concluded about our international competitive position from a systematic investigation of the past behavior of our exports and imports and those of other countries. It is hoped that his study will, among other things, throw light on the relations between our international trade and payments, on the one hand, and employment levels and growth rates at home and abroad, on the other. These relations bear on one of the major policy issues now confronting the United States—that is, the kinds of effects which higher employment and faster growth in this country would have on its balance of payments.

I am greatly indebted for criticism and encouragement in the preparation of this paper to Arthur F. Burns, who has been patient enough to read and discuss the manuscript at various stages of its development and to try to save me from serious error. I am also indebted for a careful and critical reading of the manuscript to other colleagues at the National Bureau, especially to Solomon Fabricant, Geoffrey H. Moore, Hourmouzis G. Georgiadis, Irving B. Kravis, Ilse Mintz, and Norman B. Ture; and, among the members of the Board of Directors, to Erwin D. Canham, Crawford H. Greenewalt, Gottfried Haberler, and Willard L. Thorp. My thanks are due H. Irving Forman for drawing the charts, James F. McRee, Jr., for editing the manuscript, and Alice Goldwasser, Elias Logos, and Esther Reichner for helping in the preparation of some of the statistical and other materials.

My sense of obligation is also very great to my old friends and colleagues at the U.S. Department of Commerce, particularly to Walther Lederer and his staff in the Balance of Payments Division. Though having no responsibility for the analysis which I have attempted and, indeed, disagreeing on some questions of balance-of-payments presentation of special concern to them, they have generously provided me with supplementary data and helpful advice on many points. Like everyone else interested in the problems considered here, I am above all indebted to them for their contributions to knowledge about our international trade and payments position.

Many others have been generous with their time and ideas, and sometimes with their criticisms and dissents, in reviewing my drafts or in responding to my queries and requests for help. Though I must absolve them of any responsibility for or concurrence in my analysis, I especially want to thank Oscar L. Altman, Philip Arnow, Carl P. Blackwell, Jack Downie, Peter Fousek, Irving S. Friedman, Milton Gilbert, Frances Hall, Seymour E. Harris, Arthur B. Hersey, Edward S. Lynch, Alfred Maizels, Robert J. Myers, Evelyn Parrish, William A. Salant, Christopher T. Saunders, Robert W. Stevens, and Robert Triffin.

HAL B. LARY

Chapter I

Introduction and Summary: Problems Posed by the Balance-of-Payments Deficit

1. *Doubts Regarding Our Competitive Strength*

It is something of a paradox that doubt should arise concerning the competitive strength of a country which, during the two and three-quarters years ended September 1962, had an export surplus averaging $5 billion on its foreign merchandise trade, or $7.2 billion including nonmilitary services. It is still a large surplus if one excludes from exports close to $2.5 billion of goods and services directly paid for by the United States Government, such as farm products supplied as economic aid to other countries under our surplus disposal programs.

Nevertheless, doubt has arisen about our competitive strength and, therewith, about the soundness of our international financial position. The reason is that, even at these high levels, our surplus on goods and nonmilitary services fails to cover our military expenditures abroad, government aid programs, private long-term investments, and transfers of personal remittances and pensions. To finance these items, net of corresponding payments to us, we need at present levels of operations a surplus on goods and nonmilitary services of something like $8.5 billion each year (Chart 1). The amount required is much greater if, in addition, it must cover outflows of short-term capital of the magnitude experienced in 1960 and 1961.

Any shortfall in the surplus on goods and nonmilitary services in relation to these various expenditures and transfers has to be made up by sales from our gold stock or additions to foreign dollar balances and other liquid claims on the United States. It is, in fact, these latter items—changes in our gold holdings and total liquid liabilities—that

1

CHART 1

United States Balance of Payments,
Annual Averages for January 1960-September 1962

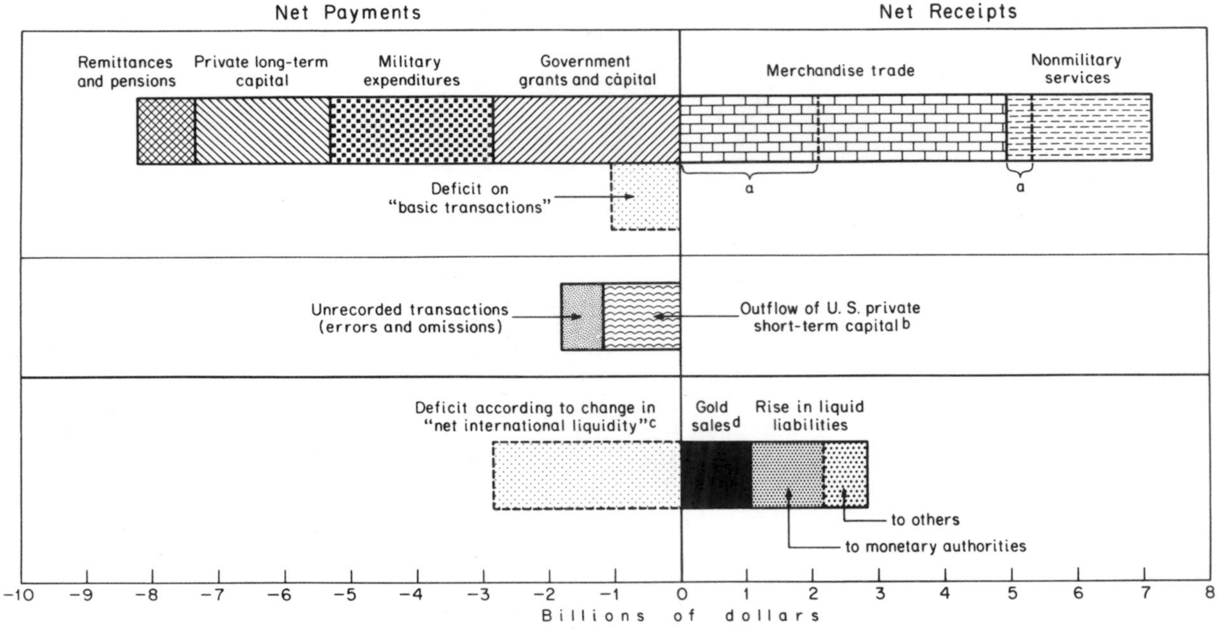

Net Receipts

Net Payments

Nonmilitary services

Merchandise trade

a

a

Government grants and capital

Military expenditures

Private long-term capital

Remittances and pensions

Deficit on "basic transactions"

Outflow of U. S. private short-term capital b

Unrecorded transactions (errors and omissions)

Gold sales d

Rise in liquid liabilities

to others

to monetary authorities

Deficit according to change in "net international liquidity"c

Billions of dollars

-10 -9 -8 -7 -6 -5 -4 -3 -2 -1 0 1 2 3 4 5 6 7 8

Problems Posed by the Payments Deficit

are taken by the Commerce Department as representing the change in our "net international liquidity," shown in Chart 1, and as measuring the deficit or surplus in the balance of payments. As will be discussed later, however, the balance on "basic transactions," also shown in the chart, or some other combination of the items may provide a more meaningful measure of the deficit or surplus.

Clearly, then, the adequacy of our competitive strength has to be judged in relation to the size of the burdens to be borne, and corrective adjustments may take the form either of reducing the size of these burdens or of increasing the size of the surplus on goods and nonmilitary services. These two magnitudes are, of course, by no means wholly independent of each other. Looked at very broadly, private foreign investment and the Government's operations abroad add to the ability of other countries to acquire our goods and services. Sometimes the link is very close—for instance, when foreign aid is directly embodied in gifts of food or otherwise tied to procurement in the United States. In such cases a reduction in our expenditures may mean a more or less equivalent reduction in our receipts.[1] In other cases, however, the

[1] Transfers in kind (other than military items supplied as grants-in-aid) are treated in the United States balance of payments as if the funds were first paid over to foreign account (i.e., a "payment") and then used to buy from us the exports in question (i.e., a "receipt"). This treatment has the advantage of covering movements of real resources, and not financial transactions only, but it tends to make the balance-of-payments impact of the foreign aid program, on the one hand, and our export earnings, on the other, appear greater than they actually are. The impact on the balance of payments would not be nil, however, unless the goods supplied under the aid program consisted exclusively of things which the beneficiary country would not otherwise have purchased from the United States.

3

connection is remote, as would be true of military expenditures or private investments in countries which are otherwise well supplied with dollars. The problem of strengthening the balance of payments may therefore be thought of as one of increasing receipts or reducing payments in ways which are not offset by their effects on other balance-of-payments items but yield a net reduction in the deficit.

A balance-of-payments deficit is not, in itself, proof of competitive inadequacy. One would need to know more about the causes and prospects. The longer a deficit continues, however, the more it would seem to. point to some fundamental difficulty, and 1962 has marked our fifth successive year of substantial deficit. Indeed, some would stress in this regard that the United States has been in deficit ever since 1950 except for brief intervals during the Korean war and again during the Suez crisis.[2] That rather overstates the duration of our problem. The deficits shown in the balance of payments prior to the Suez crisis were small, on the whole, in relation to our reserves, useful in strengthening those of other countries (Chart 2), and not such as to seem to require urgent collective policies.

After the Suez interlude, the deficits reappeared in much greater size. On the definition employed by the Commerce Department, they ranged between $3.5 billion and $4 billion annually in 1958, 1959 and 1960 and, though declining to $2.5 billion in 1961 and to an annual rate of $1.9 billion in the first nine months of 1962, have produced cumulatively unwelcome effects on our net international reserve position.

Out of these protracted deficits arises the fear that, at prevailing rates of exchange, our competitive position is not strong enough to yield a tolerable balance in our international transactions except perhaps at a level of domestic economic activity lower than would be consistent with our other objectives at home and abroad. How much relief a compression of domestic activity affords to the United States balance of payments is, moreover, in doubt. Whatever is gained by reducing imports or releasing resources for export may be offset by adverse repercussions on the buying power of neighboring countries closely dependent on the United States market and by the enhanced attraction, to Americans and others, of investing in Europe and other more rapidly growing areas.

[2] See Table 1, pp. 12, 13.

4

CHART 2

Gold Reserves of the United States and Holdings of Gold and Dollars by Other Countries and International Agencies

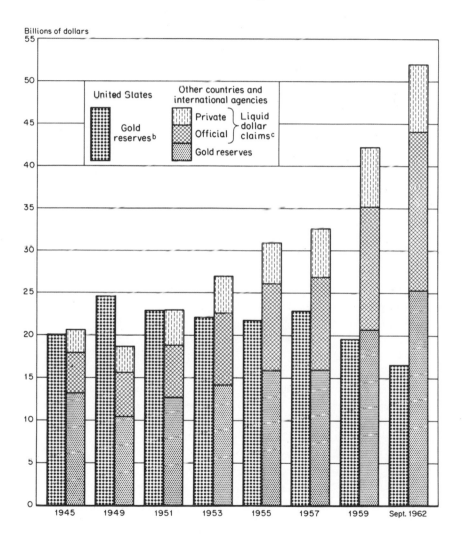

a Data for end of year or month.

b Figure for end of September 1962 includes $450 million of foreign convertible currencies.

c Includes short-term liabilities to foreigners reported by banks in the United States and also foreign holdings of U.S. Government long-term securities. The latter cannot be broken down between "official" and "private," and are here allocated to the first category on the basis of partial data indicating that the greater part of these securities are so held.

SOURCE: Federal Reserve Board and U.S. Department of Commerce.

2. *The New Balance-of-Payments Constraint*

The United States thus finds itself exposed to an unfamiliar and awkward constraint. Policies with respect to foreign trade, economic assistance to the less developed countries, military cooperation, and private foreign investment come under closer scrutiny for their effects on the balance of payments. Our effort to attune the commercial policies of the United States and the Common Market seems to be inspired not only by a desire to benefit by freer trade but perhaps even more by a concern lest preferential trading arrangements among other countries add to the stresses in our international payments position.

Questions arise also with regard to the balance-of-payments effects of domestic economic policies. Monetary and fiscal policies aimed at countering recession or at stimulating long-term growth now have to be framed with an eye to their external as well as their internal repercussions. Conflict has already been experienced between domestic objectives and the external stability of the dollar. The dollar itself is no longer immune to speculative attack.

The balance of payments has become, in the words of President Kennedy, "one of the key factors in our national economic life,"[3] and strengthening the balance of payments has become a major objective so as to widen the scope for other policy action.

Even if the balance-of-payments deficit were soon to be overcome, the United States could scarcely regain the degree of freedom from external constraint which it had previously known behind the shield of the dollar shortage. For several decades, foreign countries' demands for dollars had usually been greater, frequently far greater, than their current dollar receipts. This disparity did not repose, as many came to

[3] Message on Balance of Payments and Gold, February 6, 1961.

believe, on some unyielding structural disequilibrium causing a permanent dollar shortage. It derived rather from the extraordinary concatenation of misfortunes that befell the world over this period. These included two world wars with their heavy demands for supplies from the United States and a reduction in other countries' export possibilities, followed in each case by urgent relief and reconstruction needs and monetary disturbances abroad. In between came the Great Depression, marked by the shriveling of United States import demand and the drawing down of American investments abroad, and then the flight of European capital to the United States as the Second World War approached.

The dollar thus came to be looked upon as being chronically in short supply. By the end of World War II, it had acquired a status scarcely distinguishable from that of gold and indeed, when United States reserves reached their peak in 1949, was backed by 70 per cent of the world's monetary gold outside the Soviet Union.[4] Now, with the disappearance of some of the earlier disparities, the shift in the United States balance of payments to large deficits, the consequent fall in its gold stocks and rise in its liquid liabilities, and the increased international mobility of private capital, the United States is concerned not only about its competitive strength as a world trader but also about its problems as a world banker.

3. Some Tentative Findings

From the standpoint of our international objectives, the problem posed by the balance of payments may be regarded as one of increasing our competitive strength or else reducing the demands made upon it. With respect to our domestic objectives, the problem may be viewed as one of achieving greater freedom from external constraint in the pursuit

[4] The dollar fulfilled, in postwar international finance, the classical textbook functions of money. It was the "unit of account" conveniently specified in many international financial and commercial agreements, even among members of the Communist bloc. It was a universally acceptable "medium of exchange," and working balances of dollars were accordingly needed for international settlements. And, because these advantages were expected to endure, the dollar became a widely used "standard of deferred payments" and was eagerly sought as a "store of value" by central banks, commercial banks, business firms, and individuals.

of economic stability, long-term growth of output, and higher employment. To the extent that we solve the first problem, we facilitate solutions to the second. And to the extent that we can select and apply domestic policies in ways which strengthen our international position rather than impose new strains, we also facilitate solutions to the first problem.

Some of those who are most skeptical about the first problem or most impatient about the second have tended to doubt that these objectives can be reconciled without abandoning the further objective of maintaining the dollar at its present foreign exchange value. Speculative activity of varying intensity in the foreign exchange and gold markets has reflected the same doubt. A change could take the form of a devaluation to a new fixed gold parity—on the doubtful assumption that other countries would, in fact, be willing to see their currencies and export prices rise in relation to our own. Or, as a number of students of monetary problems would prefer, the dollar might be freed from any fixed ties to gold or other currencies—a panacea to some but Pandora's box to many others. Reasons for doubting that the United States will need to follow either of these courses will be offered in the present essay. Here, by way of a partial summary in advance, it may be suggested that the more pessimistic views entertained with regard to the future of the balance of payments and the dollar may need to be modified for several reasons.

First of all, views on the present position of the United States in the world economy still seem to be permeated by the experience of 1958 and 1959, when the balance of payments abruptly shifted to a deficit of alarming proportions. This shift undoubtedly reflected certain major changes in the conditions of international competition, attributable to developments both at home and abroad, but was greatly accentuated by various circumstances of a more ephemeral nature which, even now, are not always adequately taken into account.

Second, impressions of a fundamental deficiency in our competitive power were enlivened by the new element introduced into our international accounts in 1960 and 1961 with the heavy outflow of liquid capital and by the fact that, on the Commerce Department's method of reckoning, these flows were not as clearly distinguished as they might have been from other more basic factors contributing to the deficit. The informed observer, with time to study the Commerce Department's presentation and analysis, had no difficulty in making this distinction.

Others, including many most concerned about our international position, were not equally well placed to do so. With the subsidence of these liquid capital outflows in the first half of 1962—largely a reflection of the currency difficulties experienced by Canada—the reverse risk arose that the extent of the basic improvement in the balance of payments would be exaggerated for a time in public opinion. The pendulum swung back once more in the second half of the year with renewed large outflows of liquid funds.

Third, appraisals of the balance of payments sometimes make little allowance for the time element in adjustments to balance-of-payments disturbances. A country's strength in international competition is not to be judged only by its external deficit or surplus, however that may be measured, but also in relation to the nature and degree of the disturbances experienced and to the rate at which they are offset. Adjustments to such major changes as those which have occurred in the world economy during the past decade could not be easy and instantaneous, especially with the downward rigidity of costs and prices characteristic of modern industrial societies. In the light of these considerations it deserves to be stressed that the United States has, in fact, increased its exports of goods and nonmilitary services appreciably faster than its imports, not only since 1959 but also in relation to their respective levels at the beginning of the 1950's. These results are subject to important qualifications, as will be seen, and may be attributable only in part to specific processes of adjustment, whether policy-determined or otherwise, set in motion by the disturbances experienced. They nevertheless seem to point to some significant elements of strength in our competitive position and, in conjunction with the gradual fruition of the various corrective measures which have been taken, suggest that the balance-of-payments problem may be solved without recourse to extreme measures.

The first of the above points, concerning the combination of circumstances which produced the large deficits of 1958 and 1959, will be clarified by the sketch of balance-of-payments developments since the war given in Chapter II. The second, concerning the role of short-term capital movements and the problems which they present for analysis and policy, will be introduced in that chapter and further considered in Chapter IV. The third point—that is, the disturbances experienced in the United States balance of payments, the extent to which they have been offset, and some of the problems and uncertainties which lie ahead—will be developed in Chapter III and in the first section of Chapter IV.

Against this background, Chapter IV considers the possibilities of improving processes of adjustment in the balance of payments. It suggests that, whatever may be done in this direction, periods of disturbance and strain are to be expected in a rapidly changing world and that time must be allowed for adjustments to be made in an orderly manner. The need is therefore seen of enlarging the resources available to tide over such periods and to prevent strains in confidence such as those which have troubled the last several years. It is further suggested that this need may be especially great for the United States not merely because of its role as the major international reserve center but also because of certain distinctive features of its economy which tend to make external adjustments slower than in other countries more closely integrated into world trade. Because of the special position of the United States in these respects, its problems are not to be confused with the vaguer and less acute questions which have been raised with regard to the adequacy of international liquidity in general. To meet its own problems without, however, reducing international liquidity, the United States may need to aim at achieving not just a balance but a surplus in its international transactions to be settled by the accumulation of foreign convertible currencies rather than by reductions in the gold and dollar assets of other countries.

Chapter II

Sketch of the Balance of Payments
Since the War

An appraisal of our international payments position needs to take account of the way it has evolved in recent years and of the varied forces which have shaped its development. The point of central interest is the size and persistence of the deficit. Section 1 of this chapter traces the course of the deficit over the postwar period and considers some of its cumulative effects, and is also concerned with the concept of the deficit and how the deficit appears according to alternative methods of measurement.[1] Section 2 reviews our balance-of-payments experience more broadly and relates developments in our foreign trade and other transactions to the course of events in the United States economy and in the rest of the world. Section 3 discusses the problem of making valid generalizations about our balance-of-payments position and how it has altered over the postwar period.

1. *The Concept and Evolution of the Deficit*

DISTINCTION BETWEEN LIQUID CAPITAL MOVEMENTS AND OTHER TRANSACTIONS

The approach taken here reflects the view that it is useful to distinguish flows of liquid capital from other transactions in the balance of payments. In recent years, liquid funds have proved to be extremely mobile, as evidenced by the data given in Table 1 on the large recorded flows of United States and foreign private short-term capital

[1] For a fuller discussion of concepts and methods of measurement of the balance of payments, see Appendix A.

TABLE 1

EVOLUTION OF THE DEFICIT IN THE U.S. BALANCE OF PAYMENTS
ON THREE CONCEPTS

(millions of dollars)

Period	Deficit (—) on Basic Trans- actions[a] (1)	Recorded Net Outflow (—) of U.S. Private Short-Term Capital[b] (2)	Unrecorded Trans- actions (errors and omissions) (3)	Deficit (—) on Commerce Department's Definition (1+2+3)[c] (4)
1950	— 3,432	— 127	— 21	— 3,580
1951	— 717	— 65	477	— 305
1952	— 1,599	— 48	601	— 1,046
1953	— 2,608	117	339	— 2,152
1954	— 1,054	— 669	173	— 1,550
1955	— 1,461	— 187	503	— 1,145
1956	— 1,021	— 457	543	— 935
1957	— 449	— 188	1,157	520
1958	— 3,655	— 362	488	— 3,529
1959	— 4,232	77	412	— 3,743
	(— 4,667)[h]			(— 4,178)[h]
1960	— 1,900	—1,433	— 592	— 3,925
1961	— 527	—1,332	— 602	— 2,461
	(— 1,216)[h]			(— 3,150)[h]
1962[i]	— 573	— 626	— 696	— 1,895
	(— 1,302)[h]			(— 2,624)[h]
Quarters[j]				
1960 I	— 581	— 103	4	— 680
II	— 375	— 260	— 140	— 775
III	— 443	— 555	— 159	— 1,157
IV	— 501	— 515	— 297	— 1,313
1961 I	116	— 406	— 29	— 319
II	858	— 316	— 366	176
	(134)[h]			(— 548)[h]
III	— 868	— 235	193	— 910
	(— 793)[h]			(— 835)[h]
IV	— 633	— 375	— 400	— 1,408
	(— 673)[h]			(— 1,448)[h]
1962 I	— 268	— 314	106	— 476
II	— 110	18	— 134	— 226
	(— 186)[h]			(— 302)[h]
III[p]	— 52	— 173	— 494	— 719
	(— 523)[h]			(— 1,190)[h]
Cumulative totals				
1950-1962[k]	—23,085	—5,143	2,956	—25,272
1950-1957	—12,341	—1,624	3,772	—10,193
1958-1962[k]	—10,744	—3,519	— 816	—15,079

(continued)

TABLE 1 (concluded)

Period	Increase in U.S. Liquid Liabilities^d to Other Than Foreign Monetary Authorities		Deficit (—) on Official Settlements Basis (4+5+6)e (7)	Increase in U.S. Liquid Liabilities^d to Foreign Monetary Authorities^f (8)	Gold Sales or Purchases (—) by the United States^g (9)
	Commercial Banks (5)	Other (6)			
1950	303	— 35	— 3.312	1,569	1,743
1951	498	345	538	—485	— 53
1952	31	193	— 822	1,201	—379
1953	— 59	107	— 2,104	943	1,161
1954	— 41	68	— 1,523	1,225	298
1955	414	— 10	— ·741	700	41
1956	419	255	— 261	567	—306
1957	50	575	1,145	—347	—798
1958	48	454	— 3,027	752	2,275
1959	1,140	320	— 2,283 (— 2,718)h	1,552	731
1960	104	257	— 3,564	1,862	1,702
1961	615	587	— 1,259 (— 1,948)h	517	742
1962i	— 60	387	— 1,689 (— 2,418)h	979	710
*Quarters*j					
1960 I	457	— 19	— 203	153	50
II	132	203	— 556	462	94
III	5	— 47	— 1,233	596	637
IV	—490	120	— 1,572	651	921
1961 I	— 19	— 55	— 382	36	346
II	414	156	659 (— 65)h	—329	—330
III	154	80	— 675 (— 600)h	405	270
IV	66	406	— 861 (— 901)h	405	456
1962 I	429	263	230	—420	190
II	—256	246	— 322 (— 398)h	529	—207
IIIp	—218	—219	— 1,175 (— 1,646)h	625	550
Cumulative totals					
1950-1962k	3,477	3,406	—18,480	10,790	7,690
1950-1957	1,615	1,498	— 7,080	5,373	1,707
1958-1962k	1,862	1,908	—11,400	5,417	5,983

NOTES TO TABLE 1

ᵃ Goods and services (including military expenditures), government grants and capital, and private long-term investment.

ᵇ Less net inflow of funds through changes in foreign commercial credits to the United States (these changes being netted out in column 2 rather than included in columns 5 and 6 in order to conform to the Commerce Department's present method of calculating the deficit).

ᶜ Equals, with signs reversed, sum of columns 5, 6, 8, and 9. But see notes i and j.

ᵈ As defined by the Commerce Department, liquid liabilities include foreign holdings of deposits, U.S. Treasury bills and certificates, bankers' acceptances, commercial paper, and other short-term claims on the United States (and also foreign holdings of U.S. government bonds) as reported by banks in the United States, government agencies, and nonfinancial concerns (i.e., exporters, importers, and industrial and commercial firms). For the years 1950-1954 it is assumed that all transactions of foreign countries in U.S. government bonds were for the account of foreign monetary authorities; thereafter an estimated division is made between these and other accounts.

ᵉ Equals, with signs reversed, sum of columns 8 and 9.

ᶠ Includes changes in U.S. liquid liabilities to the International Monetary Fund.

ᵍ Includes, beginning March 1961, changes in holdings of foreign convertible currencies by the U.S. monetary authorities.

ʰ Figures adjusted to exclude effects of unscheduled repayments of foreign obligations to the U.S. Government, as follows: 1959, $150 million in first quarter and $285 million in fourth quarter; 1961, $724 million in second quarter, of which $75 million was advanced from the third quarter, and $40 million in the fourth quarter; 1962, $76 million in the second quarter and $471 million in the third quarter.

ⁱ First nine months (preliminary data) at annual rate, seasonally adjusted except as explained in note j.

ʲ Columns 1 to 4 are seasonally adjusted. (Quarterly figures in columns 5, 6, 8, and 9 add to the amounts given in column 4 before seasonal adjustment of the latter.)

ᵏ Through third quarter of 1962.

ᵖ Preliminary data.

SOURCE: U.S. Department of Commerce.

as well as by the capital movements which may be inferred from the behavior of unrecorded transactions (that is, errors and omissions).[2] The monetary authorities are accordingly confronted with new problems because of their ability to influence the cost and availability of credit and, hence, to affect the conditions determining international flows of liquid funds.

This is not to say that variations in the size and direction of liquid capital movements are to be explained only, or mainly, by changes in relative interest rates at home and abroad. The determining conditions are varied and variable. The steps towards external ("nonresident") currency convertibility taken by most Western European countries at the end of 1958 and subsequently by Japan were especially important both in enabling their banking and business concerns to increase working balances in the United States and in removing an obstacle to the extension of American credits to these countries. Changes in the value of several leading currencies and speculation of varying intensity in these and other currencies, including the dollar, have also been important influences, along with more usual economic forces affecting the demand for credit and the flow of funds. Moreover, changes in credit conditions in different countries will have more effect on some kinds of capital flows than on others. To allow for such factors is, however, a very different matter than to conclude that—under any given set of circumstances—a change in interest rates in the United States compared with those in other financial centers would have little effect on capital flows between them or on the relative size of their credit extensions to third countries.

Other sectors of the balance of payments are subject to a different or wider range of economic forces, as in the case of foreign trade and investment, or are determined essentially by political objectives, as in the case of economic aid and military expenditures abroad. Responsibility for policies affecting these different activities is dispersed,

[2] It is usual to define liquid capital movements in terms of the characteristics of the assets acquired—that is, whether or not the assets can be turned into cash quickly and without appreciable loss. The United States monetary authorities may, however, be more concerned with keeping fresh outflows of liquid funds from becoming unduly large than with the possibility of obtaining the liquidation and return of American funds which have already been placed abroad. From this point of view, one may think of liquid capital movements as embracing more or less the whole of so-called "short-term" capital movements, and some types of "long-term" capital movements as well.

except as they are coordinated at the highest levels of government. Monetary policy has little or no effect on some of these items and influences others only indirectly and gradually through changes in incomes, prices, and profits. From the standpoint of balance-of-payments objectives, these various types of transactions tend to be slow to adjust in the desired way and sometimes act perversely. It is, however, also appropriate to describe them as "basic transactions," since their combined behavior provides a measure of the adequacy of this country's competitive strength and its ability to defend the value of its currency.

This does not mean that an even balance on basic transactions is necessarily a sufficient goal of policy. An appropriate objective in this regard would have to be determined in the light of various considerations, including views and policies with respect to the size of liquid capital flows.[3] The distinguishing feature of the latter as contrasted with basic transactions is, however, that the monetary authorities have the possibility of acting quickly so as to keep outflows of liquid funds within tolerable limits and ward off excessive demands on gold arising from this source. A solution to the payments problem need not therefore require raising the surplus on goods and services by enough to cover these flows along with all the other more stubborn burdens resting on the balance of payments.

The size of the problem presented by liquid capital flows is inadequately revealed by the data provided through the reporting network of banks and business concerns in this country. Americans may, for instance, hold deposits directly in foreign banks rather than through American banks, or buy and sell other foreign assets through channels which pass outside the reporting system. Similar possibilities exist with respect to shifts of foreign capital into and out of the United States. A clue to such transfers may be found in the balance-of-payments entry for "unrecorded transactions," though this residual item registers the net effect of all errors and omissions, wherever they may arise in the balance of payments, and could not be attributed only to unreported capital movements. The play of capital movements is, however, suggested by the sudden shift in this item after 1959. Though varying in

---

[3] The composition of liquid capital movements is also important since, depending on their nature, they may affect the availability of funds for payments on basic transactions. To take one example, further commented on below, the growth of American credits to Japan in 1960 and 1961 undoubtedly contributed to the rise in United States exports to that country.

size from year to year, it had been regularly positive in sign, indicative of net unrecorded receipts, during the whole of the period 1951 to 1959 (Table 1), and averaged some $500 million per year. It then shifted abruptly to a minus quantity of approximately $600 million in both 1960 and 1961 and even more in 1962 on the basis of data for the first nine months. This turnabout of $1.1 billion gives some reason to suppose that the large negative residuals which started in 1960 may considerably understate the amount of unreported capital outflows and their contribution to the large deficits of the last three years as measured by the Commerce Department.[4] Philip Bell, in a correlation analysis covering the period 1952-1961, found that the entry for unrecorded transactions had, in fact, varied closely with the reported movements of United States private short-term capital, and he estimated that the amount of unreported capital flow of this nature was well in excess of $1 billion in both 1960 and 1961.[5]

THE SIZE AND CUMULATIVE EFFECT OF THE DEFICIT

Table 1 shows the balance on basic transactions as here defined, comprising exports and imports of goods and services, government

[4] This reasoning presupposes that the errors and omissions which accounted for the plus residuals in the 1950's (and which could represent either an underestimate of receipts or an overestimate of payments on "recorded" transactions) have persisted on into later years, but, since 1960, have been outweighed by unrecorded capital outflows. As an alternative, or complementary, explanation, it is possible that the phenomena responsible for the residuals have now been reversed. Thus, there is good cause to think that, in the earlier period, Europeans wanting to escape exchange controls or the risk of devaluation, and Latin American dictators or others wanting to hedge against the future, acquired assets in the United States, and that they may now have ceased to do so or even shifted funds from the United States to other countries. Many such transactions would have been handled through domestic names and addresses or in other ways so that both the earlier inflows and the later outflows of funds would have escaped the reports filed by American banks and businesses on their liabilities to foreigners or other records of capital movements.

[5] Philip W. Bell, "Private Capital Movements and the U.S. Balance-of-Payments Position," in *Factors Affecting the United States Balance of Payments* (Joint Economic Committee), Washington, December 1962, pp. 395-481. Bell reports a particularly close relation between unrecorded transactions and (1) claims on Canada and Europe reported by nonfinancial concerns in the United States and (2) foreign-currency claims on Canada reported by United States banks. His study also contains a useful statement of the reasons why capital movements may fail to be caught by the reporting system. For a fuller statement of the sources of errors and omissions in the estimates, see Walther Lederer, "Measuring the Balance of Payments," American Statistical Association, *1961 Proceedings of the Business and Economics Statistics Section*, Washington, 1962, pp. 42-44.

17

grants and capital, and private long-term investment. It also shows the balance including, in accordance with the Commerce Department's practice, transfers of United States private short-term capital and unrecorded transactions. When the net flow on these latter items is inward, as was generally true of the 1950's, the adverse balance on the Commerce Department's definition is smaller than that on basic transactions. The opposite result ensues when these flows are outward, as in 1960 and 1961.

Without exhausting the range of possibilities, Table 1 presents the balance according to yet another concept—that is, on the basis of "official settlements." The rationale of this concept is that changes in liquid liabilities to foreign private holders[6] are not merely a passive consequence of the state of the United States balance of payments, as might be true of changes in the reserves of the monetary authorities, but reflect rather the positive interest of foreign commercial banks, business concerns, and other holders in increasing or, on occasion, decreasing their working balances and other liquid assets in dollars. Changes in these assets, like those in United States private short-term claims on other countries, would therefore be entered in the balance of payments before computing the deficit or surplus, leaving gold sales or purchases and changes in the liquid claims of the monetary authorities as the direct measure, with signs reversed, of the balance.

The "official settlements" measure of the balance is, however, deficient in that some central banks, in addition to their direct dollar claims on the United States, have come to hold important dollar balances through commercial banks in their own or other countries.[7] An uncertain but apparently significant part of what appears in United States sta-

[6] See Table 1, columns 5 and 6. In addition to nonbanking concerns and private individuals, column 6 includes foreign government agencies other than central banks and treasuries, and international organizations other than the International Monetary Fund.

[7] Oscar Altman estimates that the central banks and monetary authorities of twenty or twenty-five countries hold deposits of dollars or sterling (mainly dollars) outside the United States and the United Kingdom, respectively. He further estimates that these official dollar deposits account for the greater part of the dollar funds employed in the "Euro-dollar market"—that is, the multibillion-dollar international money market developed during the last four or five years by commercial banks in London, Montreal, Paris, and other financial centers for deposit and loan operations in U.S. dollar funds. See Oscar L. Altman, "Recent Developments in Foreign Markets for Dollars and Other Currencies," in *Factors Affecting the United States Balance of Payments* (Joint Economic Committee), Washington, December 1962, pp. 483-523.

tistics as liabilities to foreign commercial banks therefore really belongs to central banks. Shifts between official and private dollar accounts in the United States may occur for other reasons as well, so that it becomes difficult to assign a clear meaning to changes in these separate categories.[8]

All three concepts of the balance of payments portrayed in Table 1 are alike in showing deficits most of the time, and very large cumulative deficits, over the period 1950 through the first nine months of 1962. The cumulative deficit is largest on the Commerce Department's definition, amounting to $25.3 billion, of which $15.1 billion is accounted for by the last four and three-quarters years. The cumulative deficit on basic transactions is only moderately smaller for the whole of the period, but with rather more of it in the earlier part and some $10.7 billion in the later part. As measured by official settlements, the cumulative figure for the twelve and three-quarters years is $18.5 billion, or considerably smaller than on either of the other two bases, but that for the later part of the period is slightly larger than the deficit on basic transactions. In all cases the deficits for some of the more recent years are greater still if the figures are adjusted, as also indicated in the table, to exclude advance repayments of foreign debt to the United States Government.

As noted in Chapter I, the balance-of-payments deficits incurred prior to the Suez crisis of 1956-57 served an essential purpose in enabling other countries to rebuild their monetary reserves and in laying the basis for the subsequent restoration of currency convertibility. Under these circumstances, the deficits of that period could scarcely be regarded, even now, as early evidence of some competitive inadequacy, especially in view of the prevalence at that time of discrimination against imports from the dollar area. But they may nevertheless have contributed significantly to our subsequent difficulties by permitting the balance

[8] This problem is illustrated by the following passage from the International Monetary Fund's *Annual Report 1962*, p. 171: "Because world reserves conventionally cover only official holdings, their size is affected by transactions between the official sector and the private bank and nonbank sectors. Shifts of this sort may reach significant proportions. In December 1961, for example, the German commercial banks converted into deutsche mark foreign assets in excess of $600 million for seasonal requirements, including window dressing purposes. Most of this was reflected in an increase in the Bundesbank's net reserves. An even larger amount of such assets was deposited abroad by the commercial banks in the following month. If it had not been for this single factor, world official exchange holdings would have shown only a very small increase during 1961."

of payments to assume a structure which, with the added burdens and increased foreign competition of later years, has proved difficult to correct.

Though the deficits registered since the Suez crisis have been large by any standard, they show a rather different size and evolution according to which of the three concepts is considered. They appear largest and most stubborn on the method of measurement employed by the Commerce Department. On this basis, and adjusted to exclude debt prepayment to the United States Government, the deficit reached a peak of $4.2 billion in 1959, remained over $3 billion in 1961, and was still at an annual rate of $2.6 billion in the first nine months of 1962. On the basic transactions concept, and again adjusted to exclude debt prepayment, the deficit was as high as $4.7 billion in 1959 but fell to $1.9 billion in 1960 and to an even lower level in 1961 and 1962. Measured by official settlements, the deficit rose to a peak of more than $3.5 billion in 1960, dipped below the $2 billion level in 1961, but then rose again to a rate of $2.4 billion on the average for January–September 1962.

All three methods of measurement thus show a decline in the deficit in the last two years compared with earlier levels. The improvement has not yet gone far enough, however, to preclude a further deterioration in our reserve position. The composition of official settlements given in Table 1 is of interest in this regard. Of the cumulative total of these settlements from 1950 to 1956, about 30 per cent was in gold and the remainder in the form of increases in the liquid dollar assets of foreign and international monetary authorities. For the period 1958 through September 1962, more than 50 per cent was in gold. This change seems to suggest that, as the cumulative effect of the United States deficits and the rise in other countries' reserves, foreign monetary authorities have become more disposed to regard gold as the preferred means of receiving settlement.[9]

Evidence which runs "contrary to a so-called 'rush' to obtain gold" has been developed by Oscar Altman in an analysis of the relation

___

[9] The share of gold in official settlements could also vary, without signifying a shift in foreign preferences, if in one period gains in reserves accrued chiefly to countries which hold their reserves largely in dollars and in another period to countries which hold them predominantly in gold. For an analysis of central bank practices in this regard, see a forthcoming study by Peter B. Kenen, *Reserve-Assets Preferences of Central Banks and Stability of the Gold-Exchange Standard,* Princeton Studies in International Finance No. 10.

between United States gold movements and the size of its balance-of-payments deficit or surplus as measured by official settlements. On the basis of the relation for the period 1946 to 1961 (depicted in Chart 3), Altman found that, as long as official settlements made by the United States did not exceed $350 million per year, other countries added these receipts to their dollar balances rather than take gold, but that each increment in official settlements above that level was effected to the extent of some 55 per cent in gold.[10] It would therefore be the increased size of the United States balance-of-payments deficits after 1957 rather than a shift in foreign preferences that explains the higher proportion settled in gold.

Altman's results would not appear, however, to eliminate the hypothesis that the preferences of foreign monetary authorities have shifted toward gold. If the points for the years 1949 to 1956, designated by circles in Chart 3, are looked at in isolation from those for other years, they do not show a very clear pattern.[11] Six of the eight years form a cluster from which no dominant relation emerges, and the gold outflow for the whole of the 1949-1956 period was smaller, and that for 1958-1961 larger, than would be indicated by Altman's equation. Irrespective of whether or not there has been a shift in foreign preferences, however, the more important conclusion suggested by Altman's analysis is that the United States could scarcely expect to continue to run large deficits without further substantial gold losses.

---

[10] See Oscar L. Altman, "Quelques Aspects du Problème de l'Or," *Cahiers de l'Institut de Science Économique Appliquée*, Series R, No. 7, October 1962. With the balance-of-payments deficit defined (1) by official settlements (as in Chart 3) and (2) by official settlements plus the increase in liquid dollar holdings of foreign commercial banks, the relations found by Altman for the period 1946 to 1961 are expressed by the following equations (in billions of dollars):

$$(1) \quad \text{Gold outflow} = -0.200 + 0.566 \text{ deficit}$$
$$(2) \quad \text{Gold outflow} = -0.282 + 0.543 \text{ deficit}$$

If the years of large U.S. balance-of-payments surpluses (1946-1948) are eliminated, the corresponding equations for the period 1949 to 1961 are:

$$(1a) \quad \text{Gold outflow} = -0.284 + 0.614 \text{ deficit}$$
$$(2a) \quad \text{Gold outflow} = -0.348 + 0.580 \text{ deficit}$$

[11] As Altman indicates (see preceding note), it may be preferable to disregard the early postwar years of large United States surpluses.

CHART 3

U.S. Balance of Payments and Gold Movements, 1947 to 1961

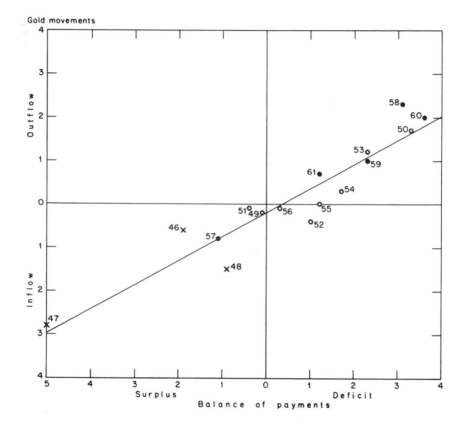

NOTE: Reproduced from data supplied by Oscar L. Altman (see note 10, Chapter 2). The balance-of-payments surplus or deficit corresponds to the "official settlements" concept, adjusted (along with the data on gold movements) to exclude gold sales to the United States by the International Monetary Fund in 1956, 1959, and 1960 for the purpose of acquiring income-earning U.S. Treasury bills and notes. The data also differ in some other respects from those given on "official settlements" in Table 1.

2. *The Changing Characteristics of the Balance of Payments*

RELIEF AND RECONSTRUCTION PERIOD, 1946-1949

In current perspective, the immediate postwar years are of interest chiefly as a reminder of the one-sided strength of the United States at that time, but they are of little use as a basis for judging the subsequent evolution of trade and payments. The dominant feature of this period was the huge excess of United States exports over imports of goods and services, totaling $32 billion for the four years 1946-1949. Exports fell off sharply after 1947, as shown in Chart 4, and a rise in the value of imports also helped to reduce the disparity but was interrupted by the 1948-49 recession in the United States.[12]

This vast export surplus was made possible chiefly by various types of public financing, including final deliveries under relief and rehabilitation programs inaugurated during the war, the special loan of $3.75 billion to the United Kingdom in 1946, Export-Import Bank loans, and the beginning of the Marshall Plan for European recovery in 1948. In addition, foreign countries liquidated gold and dollar holdings to a total of $7 billion, two-thirds of it in 1947 alone.

The payments problems of the period were aggravated by the flight of capital from other countries on the part of those wishing to escape exchange controls or the risks of devaluation. As one indication of these capital flows, unexplained receipts (errors and omissions) in the U.S. balance of payments totaled $3.1 billion from 1947 through the third quarter of 1949 and then, after the devaluation of European currencies, promptly shifted to a small outflow.

KOREAN WAR PERIOD, 1950-1952

Whether in quick response to the currency devaluation of September 1949[13] or because of an upturn in business in this country, United States imports soon began to strengthen. The great boost came, however, with the demands generated by the Korean conflict: as the result of increases in both prices and quantities, the value of United

---

[12] Balance-of-payments figures for postwar years are also given in Appendix B.

[13] The leading countries devalued as follows: United Kingdom, along with most of the overseas members of the sterling area and also Sweden, Norway, Denmark, and the Netherlands, 30.5 per cent; France, 21.8 per cent compared with the rates previously prevailing for commercial transactions; Federal Republic of Germany, 20.6 per cent; Italy, 8 per cent; Belgium, 12.3 per cent (cf. International Monetary Fund, *Annual Report 1950*, pp. 28-38).

CHART 4

U.S. Payments and Receipts on Basic Transactions Since World War II

A.   Gross Payments

a Includes remittances and pensions.

Sketch of the Balance of Payments

CHART 4 (concluded)

B. Gross Receipts

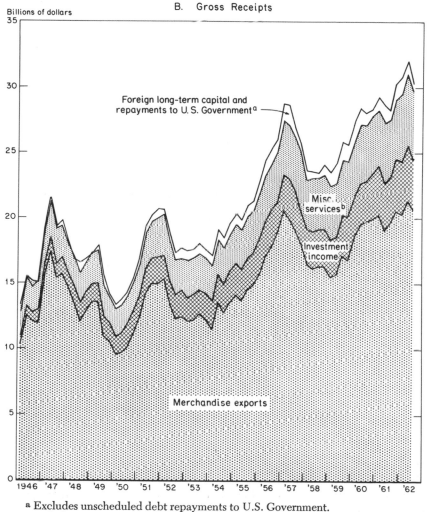

Billions of dollars

Foreign long-term capital and repayments to U.S. Government[a]

Misc. services[b]

Investment income

Merchandise exports

a Excludes unscheduled debt repayments to U.S. Government.
b Includes U.S. government receipts on military transactions.

NOTE: Quarterly data at annual rates, seasonally adjusted starting with 1950.

SOURCE: U.S. Department of Commerce (see also Appendix Tables B-1 and B-2).

States imports of goods and services rose by some 60 per cent between the fourth quarter of 1949 and the first quarter of 1951. Meanwhile, exports had risen much more slowly, and, with foreign economic aid continuing at a high level, the United States registered its first large postwar payments deficit of close to $4 billion, on the Commerce Department's definition, during the twelve months from April 1950 to March 1951.

The position then shifted once more with great rapidity. Merchandise imports weakened both in price and in volume during 1951 just after exports had begun to respond to the accumulation of purchasing power abroad. During the twelve months to March 1952, despite a growth in its military expenditures overseas, the United States registered a small balance-of-payments surplus (again on the Commerce Department basis). By the second half of 1952, however, exports also fell back with the slowing down of economic expansion in Europe and the depletion of the extraordinary buying power acquired by some of the primary producing countries at the peak of the Korean inflation.

WORLD ECONOMIC EXPANSION, 1953-1957

After a pause in 1952, economic activity in other leading industrial countries expanded strongly for five years (Chart 5), and the value of world trade rose no less than 35 per cent. The increase in United States exports was even more vigorous—some 46 per cent—and was concentrated in 1956 and 1957 as demands on the United States stemming from the investment boom abroad were reinforced by the closure of the Suez Canal.

Economic activity in the United States developed more irregularly, passing into a recession in 1953-54, rising again strongly until the end of 1956, and then turning down again in the latter part of 1957 (Chart 6). Imports of merchandise roughly paralleled the course of industrial production and rose by 22 per cent in value over the five years. Inclusive of services, the rise in imports was greater, about one-third, because of the rapid growth in United States military expenditures and tourist outlays abroad but, even so, did not keep pace with the increase in exports of goods and services.

Price increases contributed something to the rise in the value of trade in both directions and were of chief significance in steel and machinery among exports and in raw materials among imports.

CHART 5

Foreign Industrial Production and Exports of the United States and of Other Countries

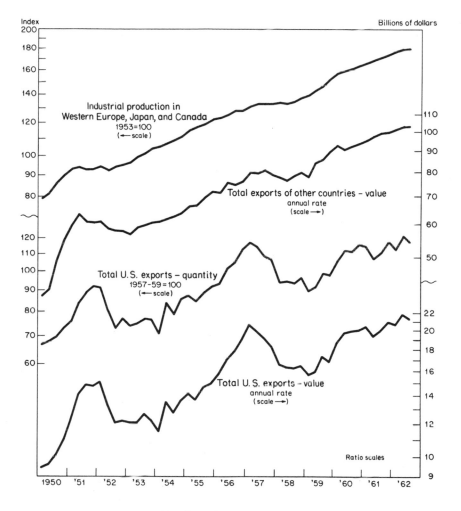

Index / Billions of dollars

Industrial production in
Western Europe, Japan, and Canada
1953=100
(←scale)

Total exports of other countries – value
annual rate
(scale→)

Total U.S. exports – quantity
1957-59=100
(←scale)

Total U.S. exports – value
annual rate
(scale→)

Ratio scales

1950 '51 '52 '53 '54 '55 '56 '57 '58 '59 '60 '61 '62

NOTE: Data are seasonally adjusted.

SOURCE: U.S. Department of Commerce, the International Monetary Fund, and the OECD.

27

CHART 6

U.S. Industrial Production and Imports

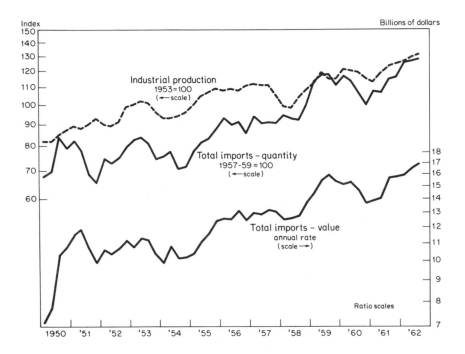

NOTE: Data are seasonally adjusted.

SOURCE: U.S. Department of Commerce, Federal Reserve Board, and the OECD.

The result of these disparities was a striking increase in the export surplus on goods and services from the post-Korean low of $400 million in 1953 to $5,750 million in 1957. There was, however, a strong offsetting, and related, increase over the period in the outflow of capital, especially into natural resource development in Canada, Latin America, and the Middle East. The deficit in the balance of payments therefore did not disappear until the 1956-57 spurt in exports,

28

and even then only momentarily. By that time, foreign exchange difficulties were being experienced by several of the major trading countries. These difficulties stemmed in part from a steep rise in imports, as in Japan and the Netherlands, and in part from the flight of capital,[14] as in the United Kingdom. In either event, policies of restraint became necessary.

THE SWOLLEN DEFICITS OF 1958 AND 1959

The second half of 1957 brought a pronounced change in the world economic climate and in United States foreign trade. In most foreign industrial countries there was only a pause or, at worst, a moderate decline in business activity as reflected in their indexes of industrial production, yet world trade reacted sharply. The fall in United States exports was especially severe from mid-1957 to mid-1958 and extended on into the following year. On the other hand, the decline in production in the United States was much more pronounced than abroad, yet its imports weakened only moderately and then, as business activity turned up earlier than in most other countries, climbed by some 25 per cent from the third quarter of 1958 to the third quarter of 1959.

Shaped first by the fall in exports and then by the rise in imports, the United States surplus on goods and services dwindled in 1958 and momentarily disappeared in the first half of 1959. The net outflow of private long-term capital fell back in 1958 from the very high 1957 level and, as credit conditions tightened in the United States, dropped still more sharply in 1959, but far from enough to offset the fall in exports. Government economic assistance, which after the end of the European Recovery Program had been going in gradually rising amounts to other areas, receded only slightly after 1957, though 1959 brought

---

[14] The importance of speculative movements is again suggested by the behavior of the residual item (errors and omissions) in the United States balance of payments, i.e., the large unidentified receipts from the third quarter of 1956 through the third quarter of 1957:

(quarterly data, seasonally adjusted, in millions of dollars)

	I	II	III	IV
1956	—15	—12	179	391
1957	448	377	363	—31

These unrecorded receipts contributed importantly to the balance-of-payments surplus in 1957, as measured by the Commerce Department, and the balance on basic transactions continued to show a deficit even in that year (Table 1).

29

the first advance repayments of foreign debt to the United States Government. The net effect was the emergence of a deficit on basic transactions of almost $3.7 billion in 1958 and $4.2 billion in 1959—$4.7 billion, in fact, exclusive of the special receipts from debt prepayments.[15]

These changes opened a new era of intensified competition for the United States, marked by the success of foreign manufacturers in penetrating the American market and in raising their share of third markets as well as by the disappearance of specific shortages abroad which had provided extraordinary outlets for many United States products during the earlier postwar years. The dramatic nature of the change was, however, greatly accentuated by a number of attendant circumstances which contributed to the exceptional rise in United States exports to a peak in early 1957 and to their exceptional fall over the next two years. The easing of boom conditions abroad, though moderate, was enough to dissipate the postwar atmosphere of scarcity and to provoke extensive liquidation of inventories of industrial materials along with some slowing down of investment activity, particularly in the extractive industries. At the same time other circumstances— including the Suez crisis, changes in United States export pricing policy for cotton, the changeover from propeller-driven to jet aircraft, and the steel strike of 1959—intensified the rise and fall in exports of petroleum, coal, and other major items.

The effects of these influences on exports can be seen in Table 2. It will be noted that the items in Groups I and II accounted for almost half of the increase in total exports from 1953-1955 to 1957 and for virtually all of the fall from 1957 to 1959. Since then, exports in the first group have shown little strength, but those in the second group returned in 1960 to the 1957 level, or approximately twice that of 1953-1955. Exports in Group III (including a number of capital goods and consumer manufactures as well as chemicals, some industrial materials, and food and accounting for over 60 per cent of total United States exports) were only lightly touched by the decline in 1958 and then increased in value to a level in 1961 more than 20 per cent higher than in 1957 and more than 70 per cent higher than in 1953-1955. On the other hand, the exports included in Group IV, headed by automo-

---

[15] The deficits in these years were, however, smaller on the Commerce Department's definition (the difference being accounted for chiefly by unrecorded transactions) and smaller still as measured by official settlements (see Table 1).

TABLE 2

U.S. EXPORTS GROUPED ACCORDING TO BEHAVIOR DURING PAST DECADE
(millions of dollars)

| | 1953-1955 (average) | 1956 | 1957 | 1958 | 1959 | 1960 | 1961 | Half-Yearly Totals | | |
								1961 Jan.-June	1961 July-Dec.	1962 Jan.-June
1. United States exports, total[a]	13,011	17,183	19,316	16,202	16,211	19,401	19,819	9,871	9,948	10,532
2. Group I, total	2,267	3,173	3,735	2,320	1,980	2,274	1,941	950	991	953
3. Iron and steel-mill products	530	763	995	563	372	611	429	200	229	212
4. Petroleum and products	667	763	993	558	480	479	445	224	221	213
5. Coal and related products	384	745	846	534	388	362	350	151	199	173
6. Tractors, trucks, and buses	686	902	901	665	740	822	717	375	342	355
7. Group II, total	1,563	2,427	3,046	2,023	1,764	3,279	3,025	1,687	1,338	1,313
8. Cotton	596	729	1,058	661	452	988	884	525	359	315
9. Iron and steelmaking raw materials	112	359	432	138	202	305	427	216	211	111
10. Nonferrous metals and materials	254	398	429	336	284	707	623	350	273	263
11. Aircraft and engines	114	170	269	217	159	551	351	228	123	223
12. Construction and mining machinery	487	771	858	671	667	728	740	368	372	401
13. Group III, total	7,453	9,634	10,437	9,900	10,520	11,789	12,814	6,203	6,611	7,100
14. Capital equipment not separately listed	1,353	2,273	2,698	2,632	2,598	3,061	3,673	1,794	1,879	2,223
15. Electrical machinery	418	513	580	564	566	574	603	306	297	325
16. Chemicals for industrial use	601	793	879	881	1,003	1,170	1,202	592	610	607
17. Consumer manufactures not separately listed	456	531	573	557	615	648	686	331	355	350
18. Industrial materials and semimanufactures not separately listed	2,276	2,780	2,969	2,717	2,942	3,233	3,298	1,566	1,732	1,678
19. Food and beverages	1,849	2,744	2,738	2,549	2,796	3,103	3,352	1,614	1,738	1,917
20. Group IV, total	1,441	1,673	1,670	1,572	1,579	1,613	1,579	807	772	878
21. Automobiles, parts, and accessories	810	982	933	846	863	899	863	439	424	516
22. Consumer appliances	232	272	273	281	266	260	267	138	129	137
23. Textile manufactures	169	171	179	166	163	176	170	91	79	86
24. Medicinals and pharmaceuticals	230	248	285	279	287	278	279	139	140	139
25. Miscellaneous items	287	276	428	387	368	446	460	224	236	288

31

NOTES TO TABLE 2

Group   I: Exports which rose strongly to 1957, fell sharply to 1959, and have not recovered earlier strength.

Group II: Exports which behaved like those in Group I to 1959 but have since regained strength.

Group III: Exports which were only moderately affected by the 1958 decline and have grown well over the period as a whole.

Group IV: Exports which were only moderately affected by the 1958 decline but have not grown much since.

ᵃ Domestic exports excluding grant-aid military equipment and supplies exported by Department of Defense under the Military Assistance Program.

SOURCE: Derived from data of the U.S. Department of Commerce.

tive products, showed little movement one way or the other over the period, and in 1961 exceeded the 1953-1955 level by less than 10 per cent.

The startling upsurge in imports in 1959 was, in large part, the result of the further penetration of the United States market by foreign manufactures and other goods, but here also the effects of temporary influences can be seen. For one thing, it is interesting to note that, of the increase of $3.1 billion from 1953-1955 to 1959 in the growth items included in Group I of Table 3, close to half came in 1959 alone. The effects of the steel strike in that year are again visible in this development. Another major influence was the upsurge in American demand for foreign automobiles to a peak in 1959, together with the continued building up of dealer outlets and stocks ahead of retail sales (Chart 7). It will also be seen that the 1959 rise in imports of Group I was reinforced, in the effect on total imports, by the strongly cyclical behavior of the items in Group II. Over the past decade as a whole, however, neither the items in Group II nor those in Group III have exhibited any significant growth. Imports of petroleum (Group IV) grew swiftly through 1958 until restrained by the imposition of import controls—an action with important balance-of-payments effects even if motivated, as it seems to have been, by other considerations.[16]

---

[16] As indicated by the data in Table 3, the import control formula adopted in 1959 did not prevent renewed increases in petroleum imports in 1961 and 1962, and apparently would have allowed a further substantial rise in 1963. On November 30, 1962, a revised formula was announced, designed to keep imports of crude oil, unfinished oil, and finished products into the United States east of the Rocky Mountains at a ratio of 12.2 per cent to domestic production (*The New York Times*, December 1, 1962).

TABLE 3

U.S. IMPORTS GROUPED ACCORDING TO BEHAVIOR DURING PAST DECADE

(millions of dollars)

	1953-55 Average	1956	1957	1958	1959	1960	1961	Half-Yearly Totals		
								1961 Jan.-June	1961 July-Dec.	1962 Jan.-June
1. *United States imports, total*[a]	10,824	12,615	12,982	12,867	15,207	14,654	14,449	6,837	7,612	7,989
2. *Group I, total*	2,024	2,799	3,253	3,689	5,117	5,034	4,799	2,112	2,687	2,753
3. Automobiles, parts, and accessories	66	147	337	547	843	612	375	181	194	253
4. Finished textile materials and manufactures	310	454	450	435	605	715	590	262	328	367
5. Consumer manufactures not separately listed	673	875	937	912	1,230	1,434	1,466	638	828	786
6. Meat and cattle	189	156	250	465	475	386	480	205	275	260
7. Alcoholic beverages	161	194	217	237	269	272	297	119	178	138
8. Capital equipment	234	368	412	481	618	602	720	326	394	419
9. Iron ore	131	251	286	233	313	322	250	95	155	151
10. Iron and steel-mill products	151	213	220	231	574	508	421	182	239	270
11. Chemicals	109	141	144	148	190	183	200	104	96	109
12. *Group II, total*	3,658	4,103	3,785	3,191	4,066	3,631	3,527	1,657	1,870	1,989
13. Building materials	390	487	407	435	603	541	538	248	290	300
14. Materials for durable goods production	2,303	2,652	2,421	1,927	2,350	2,087	1,968	892	1,076	1,103
15. Materials for nondurable goods production	965	964	957	829	1,113	1,003	1,021	517	504	586
16. *Group III, total*	4,102	4,194	4,120	4,009	4,075	4,002	3,968	2,006	1,962	2,083
17. Coffee	1,437	1,439	1,375	1,173	1,093	1,002	961	501	460	483
18. Other food not separately listed	1,315	1,297	1,333	1,482	1,527	1,549	1,520	765	755	809
19. Newsprint and paper base stocks	948	1,093	1,032	988	1,089	1,098	1,093	532	561	563
20. Materials used in agriculture	402	365	380	366	366	353	394	208	186	228
21. *Group IV (petroleum), total*	875	1,282	1,534	1,610	1,536	1,548	1,682	839	843	921
22. Miscellaneous items	165	237	290	368	414	438	473	223	250	243

NOTES TO TABLE 3

Group I: Imports which have increased sharply since 1953-1955, with especially strong impact in 1959.

Group II: Imports with pronounced cyclical behavior.

Group III: Imports showing little or no growth over the period.

Group IV: Strong growth until 1958 and forcibly restrained since.

a General imports.

SOURCE: Derived from data of the U.S. Department of Commerce

NEW STRAINS FROM CAPITAL OUTFLOWS IN 1960 AND 1961

Starting in the third quarter of 1959, exports staged a remarkable turnaround and in the second half of 1961 reached a rate somewhat higher than that achieved in the exceptional circumstances of 1957 and about 25 per cent higher than in 1958-1959. Imports performed more erratically, weakening with business activity here in the second half of 1960 and then recovering strongly again in the second half of 1961 to about the same level as two years earlier.

The renewed strength of United States exports after 1959 was largely in sales to other industrial countries, which have led the rise in world trade. As shown in Table 4, the value of exports to Western Europe and Japan averaged 90 per cent more in 1960-1961 than in 1953-1955. Exports to other countries outside the Western Hemisphere also increased substantially, though this rise is attributable in good part to United States Government assistance programs to India, Pakistan, and southeast Asia. Exports to Canada and Latin America, on the other hand, grew much less during this period and in 1960-1961 were well below the levels which had been reached in 1956-1957. The heavy weight of these Western Hemisphere countries in United States exports —far greater than their share in world trade and greater still than their share in exports of other industrial countries—could therefore be regarded as something of a drag on the development of total United States exports. The table also suggests, however, that the buying power of Canada and Latin America has suffered from the poor performance of their exports to the United States, an effect largely attributable to the general weakness of prices of primary products in the world's markets, but intensified by the failure of the United States economy to operate nearer to full-employment levels.

34

CHART 7

U.S. Imports and Retail Sales of Foreign Automobiles, 1955-1962

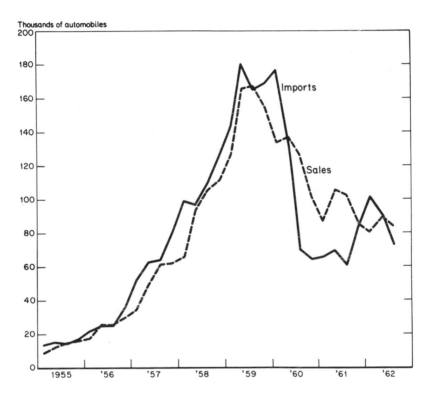

SOURCE: U.S. Department of Commerce and *Automotive News.*

Chiefly because of the strengthening of exports and the slack in imports much of the time, the deficit on basic transactions was sharply reduced to $1.9 billion in 1960 and to $1.2 billion in 1961 (exclusive of debt prepayment to the United States Government). In the first half of 1961 a small surplus was even registered, on this accounting basis, but a deficit emerged again in the second half of the year as imports recovered and as government economic assistance rose abruptly.[17]

[17] This increase was in considerable part due to capital subscriptions to international development agencies (see Table A-4).

TABLE 4
GROWTH OF WORLD AND U.S. TRADE BY AREAS, 1953-1955 TO 1960-1961

	World	Western Europe[a] and Japan	U.S.	Canada	Latin American Republics	Other Countries
I. *Growth and relative size of foreign trade turnover*[b]						
Index of value (1953-1955 = 100)						
1956-1957	126	130	131	131	115	118
1958-1959	127	134	129	125	110	120
1960-1961	149	169	143	131	114	134
Percentage of total world trade						
1953-1955	100	44.6	15.0	5.6	9.5	25.3
1960-1961	100	50.6	14.5	4.9	7.3	22.8
II. *U.S. exports to areas specified*						
Index of value (1953-1955 = 100)						
1956-1957	141	158		132	132[c]	137
1958-1959	125	131		119	120[c]	129
1960-1961	149	190		122	108[c]	167
Percentage distribution						
1953-1955	100	31.6		23.6	24.9	19.8
1960-1961	100	40.4		19.4	18.0	22.2
III. *U. S. imports from areas specified*						
Index of value (1953-1955 = 100)						
1956-1957	120	140		119	110[c]	114
1958-1959	133	188		126	107[c]	120
1960-1961	137	206		128	101[c]	126
Percentage distribution						
1953-1955	100	23.0		23.1	30.9	23.1
1960-1961	100	34.6		21.6	22.7	21.2

SOURCE: For the United States, the Department of Commerce; for Latin American Republics, International Monetary Fund (*International Financial Statistics,* September 1961 and October 1962); for other countries and country groups, OECD (*Overall Trade by Countries,* Series A, June 1962).

NOTE: Data for the United States and for total world trade exclude U.S. exports in Special Category Types I and II.

[a] European members of the OECD.

[b] Exports plus imports.

[c] Indexes of the value of U.S. trade with the Latin American republics, excluding Cuba, are as follows (1953-1955 = 100):

	1956-1957	*1958-1959*	*1960-1961*
U.S. exports	132	121	121
U.S. imports	111	106	109

It may be noted, however, that the levels of these index numbers for 1960-1961 were affected by the shift of U.S. sugar purchases away from Cuba, partly to other Latin American countries, though partly to other areas also.

Despite the notable reduction in the deficit on basic transactions after 1959, the increase in foreign gold and liquid dollar holdings through transactions with the United States (i.e., the deficit as defined by the Commerce Department) remained at the high levels of $3.9 billion in 1960 and $2.5 billion in 1961 (or $3.1 billion adjusted to exclude debt prepayments) because of the heavy recorded outflow of United States private short-term capital and recorded transfers.

Of the recorded outflow of United States private short-term funds, aggregating more than $3 billion from the beginning of 1960 through the first quarter of 1962, almost 45 per cent went to Japan (Table 5), largely in the form of trade and financial credits. The steep rise in American credits to that country, accompanied by extensive credits also from European sources operating through the "Euro-dollar" market, was occasioned by its balance-of-payments difficulties, the easing of its restrictions on external borrowing, and apparently also by the keen interest of American banks in strengthening their ties with the Japanese economy.

During the second half of 1960, the spread in interest rates between the United States and leading foreign financial centers which developed as business turned down here while expansion continued abroad led to substantial outflows of liquid funds. These operations, which added to the loss of gold and appeared to mark a turn for the worse in the United States balance of payments, sparked still other transfers attributable to a weakening of confidence in the dollar.

With regard to that part of these various credits and other transfers reported by American banks and business concerns, it is difficult to say how much they contributed to the balance-of-payments deficits of 1960 and 1961. To an appreciable extent they served to finance exports which otherwise would not have been made unless the borrowers had been able to obtain funds for this purpose from sources outside the United States. On the other hand, those outflows of liquid funds which passed outside the reporting network presumably did little to promote exports and may have contributed far more to the loss of reserves than might be judged merely from the residual item for unreported transactions. According to the estimates previously noted,[18] these unrecorded capital transfers may have approached in size the recorded flows in 1960 and 1961 as reported by American banks and business enterprises.

[18] Page 17.

TABLE 5

REPORTED U.S. PRIVATE SHORT-TERM CLAIMS ON FOREIGN COUNTRIES

(millions of dollars)

	1960 Calendar Year	1961 Calendar Year	Increase or Decrease (—) 1962			Amount Outstanding June 30, 1962
			First Quarter	Second Quarter	Third Quarter	
Total reported by banks and nonfinancial concerns in the U.S.[a]	1,341	1,435	312	—103	61	6,491
DISTRIBUTION BY COUNTRY						
Major financial centers, total	603	511	68	—167	144	2,076
United Kingdom	343	—137	—23	—38	32	316
Common Market and Switzerland	52	195	21	—12	—13	666
Canada	208	453	70	—117	125	1,094
Other countries, total	738	924	244	64	—83	4,415
Japan	491	662	255	—22	—46[b]	1,776
Latin American Republics	186	135	9	24	—53[b]	1,762
Other countries	61	127	—20	62	—7[b]	877
DISTRIBUTION BY CURRENCY						
Payable in U.S. dollars, total	931	1,349	409	—109	—83[b]	5,749
Payable in foreign currencies, total	410	86	—97	6	—6[b]	742
Major financial centers	371	46	—87	—17	—14[b]	569
Other countries	39	40	—10	23	8[b]	173

[a] Excludes holdings of the Exchange Stabilization Fund.
[b] As reported by banks only.

SOURCE: U.S. Department of Commerce.

THE BALANCE OF PAYMENTS IN 1962

On the surface, the balance of payments appeared to strengthen encouragingly during the first half of 1962 and then to deteriorate alarmingly once more in the third quarter. These abrupt shifts were, however, largely attributable to short-run disturbances, including, in particular, those associated with the depreciation and stabilization of the Canadian dollar. These disturbances affected various components of the balance of payments, including the timing of merchandise exports and imports, but seem to have had an especially marked impact on recorded short-term capital movements and on unrecorded transactions. The variations from quarter to quarter were accordingly much more violent in the deficit as measured by the Commerce Department than in the deficit on basic transactions, as shown by the following figures from Table 1 (quarterly, seasonally adjusted, in millions of dollars):

		1962	
	1961[a]	I	II	III[b]
Deficit (—) on basic transactions	—132	—268	—110	— 52
Less: Debt prepayments	172	—	76	471
Deficit on basic transactions, exclusive of debt prepayments	—304	—268	—186	— 523
Add: Recorded outflow (—) of U.S. private short-term capital[c]	—333	—314	18	— 173
Unrecorded transactions	—150	106	—134	— 494
Deficit on Commerce Department's definition, exclusive of debt prepayments	—787	—476	—302	—1,190

[a] Quarterly rate.
[b] Preliminary.
[c] Less changes in foreign commercial credits to the United States.

In view of these wide and partly offsetting swings in the quarterly data, it is probably best to take the consolidated results for the nine months as a guide to the recent status of the balance of payments. These results, expressed as annual rates, are given in Table 6 along with annual averages for earlier periods. It will be noted that the deficit on basic transactions, exclusive of receipts from debt prepayments, was at a rate of $1.3 billion, or somewhat less than the 1960-1961 average. There was an even larger reduction in the deficit as computed by the Commerce Department, though, at a rate of $2.6 billion, it remained much higher than the deficit on basic transactions, for reasons partly hidden in unrecorded transactions.

Gross payments and gross receipts both rose to new high levels in 1962. Compared with the two preceding years, the principal increases in payments were in merchandise imports and in government economic aid. The increases in the latter contributed, however, to the rise in merchandise exports. Receipts were also buoyed up by the continued rapid growth in income from foreign investments. Another important contribution was military cash receipts by the United States Government, including foreign official funds set aside at the Treasury during the period against future orders and deliveries. Actual deliveries of military goods and services during the nine months were only about 60 per cent as large as total cash receipts, and it is still too early to judge what the future course of this item will be.

A question of major current interest concerns the effect which a higher level of employment and production in the United States would have on imports and other items in the balance of payments. It was noted above that the reduction in the deficit on basic transactions after 1959 owed a good deal to the weakening of United States import demand during the 1960-61 recession. Some ground for encouragement may be found in the fact that the further reduction of the deficit during 1962 was achieved along with a significantly higher level of business activity in this country. Reference to Table 3 shows that a marked cyclical upturn in imports of industrial materials contributed importantly to the rise in total imports. At the same time imports of consumer manufactures (other than automobiles) and capital equipment continued to make impressive gains. It is noteworthy that the impact of these developments on the trade balance was not more unfavorable than it was, all the more so since exports to Japan fell off sharply after the end of 1961 following measures taken by the Japanese authorities to protect reserves and the drying up of new American credits to Japan after the first quarter of 1962. It may be that this reduction has run its course, now that Japan has been able to register some increase in its reserves. The commodity detail given in Table 2 indicates that exports of capital equipment continued during 1962 to provide the main impetus to the growth in exports and suggests that the further growth of the export total may depend heavily on the maintenance of a high rate of investment activity in foreign countries.[19]

[19] Exports of foodstuffs also showed large gains, part of which may be attributable to aid shipments and to temporary influences (including drought conditions affecting foreign grain supplies and efforts by exporters to land shipments ahead of the Common Market restrictions which became effective at the beginning of August 1962). The exceptionally high level of these exports may, however, be set off against the unusually low level of cotton exports, as foreign buyers awaited an expected reduction in the export price of cotton by the Department of Agriculture.

TABLE 6

U.S. BALANCE OF PAYMENTS BY SELECTED PERIODS, 1953 TO 1962
(billions of dollars, annual averages or annual rates)

	1953-1955	1956-1957	1958-1959	1960-1961	1962 Jan.-Sept.
I. Basic transactions					
U.S. payments, recorded:	20.6	26.8	28.4	30.2	32.4
Merchandise imports	11.0	13.0	14.1	14.6	16.1
Military expenditures	2.7	3.1	3.3	3.0	3.0
Other services	3.1	4.1	4.7	5.4	5.7
Remittances and pensions	.6	.7	.8	.9	.9
Government grants and capital outflows	2.4	3.0	3.1	3.7	4.3
U.S. private long-term capital	.9	2.9	2.5	2.5	2.3
U.S. receipts, recorded:					
Including debt prepayments	18.9	26.1	24.5	28.9	31.8
Excluding debt prepayments			24.2	28.6	31.1
Merchandise exports	13.1	18.4	16.3	19.7	20.8
Military sales	.2	.3	.3	.4	.9ᵃ
Investment income	2.2	2.7	2.9	3.5	4.0
Other services	2.7	3.6	3.8	4.0	4.4
Repayments on U.S. Government loans					
Ordinary repayments	.5	.6	.6	.7	.6
Special prepayments	—	—	.2	.3	.7
Foreign long-term investment in U.S.	.3	.5	.4	.4	.4
Balance on basic transactions:					
Including debt prepayments	—1.7	—.7	—3.9	—1.2	— .6
Excluding debt prepayments			—4.2	—1.5	—1.3
II. Private short-term capital movements and unrecorded transactions					
Recorded U.S. short-term capitalᵇ	— .2	—.3	— .1	—1.4	— .6
Unrecorded transactions	.3	.8	.4	— .6	— .7
Balance corresponding to Commerce Department definition:					
Including debt prepayments	—1.6	—.2	—3.6	—3.2	—1.9
Excluding debt prepayments			—3.9	—3.5	—2.6

41

ᵃ Includes deliveries on military sales during the period and $360 million (annual rate) transferred to restricted accounts with the U.S. Treasury against military purchases to be made by foreign countries.

ᵇ Less changes in foreign commercial credits to the United States.

NOTE: Detail may not add to totals shown because of rounding.

SOURCE: U.S. Department of Commerce.

3. *The Selection of Periods for Comparison*

This brief review of the shifting postwar scene underscores the difficulty of making valid generalizations about our international payments position and how it has altered during this time. Statements about the "present" and how it has changed from the "past" are likely to be influenced by the particular constellation of forces operating at one time or another, some of which are more ephemeral than others. How, then, can one sort out from the rest the more basic changes embodied in the statistical record of our balance-of-payments experience?

A usual way of trying to meet such problems is to draw averages for some base period and some terminal period, each long enough to even out the effects of erratic influences and other abnormalities, and thus permit comparisons between them without undue risk of distortion. Such a method is difficult to apply to the relatively recent developments considered here,[20] especially when it is a question of characterizing the current status of the balance of payments. There is no "terminal period" marking an end to the phenomena considered, the most recent data serve as only a rough guide to the near future, and averages could not be extended back more than a few years without risk of concealing the very disturbances and adjustments of the past decade which need to be identified. This difficulty is all the greater in that one could scarcely include the developments of 1958 and 1959 without including also those

[20] Some comparisons with prewar periods are given in the next chapter (Chart 9), but it has to be remembered that the decade immediately preceding the war was perhaps even more disturbed than that immediately afterward because of the Great Depression, exchange depreciation, trade controls, and the flight of capital to the United States.

of the preceding year or so, to which they were in considerable part a reaction. For the current picture, it therefore seems best to concentrate on the more recent figures and to introduce such qualifications as seem appropriate for the effects of cyclical or erratic influences on them.

The choice of an "initial" or base period, on the other hand, is less circumscribed, though here also one would not wish to include any of the years 1956 to 1959, nor to go back into the distorted relations immediately following the war. One possibility would be to include the whole of the intervening period, that is, the six years 1950 to 1955. This period, starting just after the European currency devaluations of 1949, includes all of the Korean episode, with effects first unfavorable and then favorable on the United States balance of payments, as well as the 1952 pause in Europe and the 1953-54 recession and ensuing recovery in the United States. The inclusion of the Korean war experience is, however, open to question, and the shorter period 1953-1955 will therefore be used in this study as the principal base of comparison. In fact, as will be seen in the next chapter, the relative changes in the major components of the balance of payments are much the same whether one takes the longer or the shorter period as a base. Nor is there much difference in the size of the initial handicap presented by the balance-of-payments deficits during the two periods, which averaged $1.8 billion for 1950-1955 and $1.7 billion for 1953-1955.

Chapter III

Elements of Strength and Weakness in Basic Transactions

---

1. *The Risk of Overexplaining the Balance of Payments*

The belief in a chronic dollar shortage continued to be widely held until long after the United States balance of payments had shifted, at the beginning of the 1950's, to a deficit. The persistence of this view is not so strange as may sometimes appear. The new deficits were not ignored, but they seemed to repose on uncertain foundations: United States military forces and expenditures abroad, which reached high levels during the Korean war, might again recede as rapidly as they had after World War II; economic aid to Europe had been completed and aid to the less developed countries had not yet been widely accepted as a regular, if not also growing, obligation; the receptivity of the United States to increased foreign competition in its own market remained subject to test; many countries in Europe and elsewhere still thought it necessary to impose quantitative restrictions against imports from the United States.

Under these circumstances, a judgment at that time that the dollar shortage had ended was not, as may now appear, a conclusion emerging unequivocally from the currently reported balance-of-payments figures, but involved an assessment and forecast of the underlying causal forces at work, political as well as economic.[1] It is not surprising that attitudes and expectations differed. The very increases which some countries were able to achieve in their reserves as a counterpart to the United States payments deficits during the pre-Suez period could be taken as evidence of their continuing hunger for dollars.

What is strange is not so much the general failure to recognize earlier that the dollar shortage had ended. It is rather the strength of the widely held view that it might never end, that it reflected some kind of enduring structural advantage on the part of the United States, and that corrective adjustments would be difficult or impossible to achieve.[2] Among the elements deemed to account for the superiority of the United States and the strength of its international payments

---

[1] For example, it was common practice in the mid-fifties to treat United States military expenditures abroad as "extraordinary." Thus, the seventh Annual Report of the OEEC showed, for the member countries combined, during 1954-55 a surplus of $1.4 billion, including military receipts from North America, but a deficit of $600 million if these receipts were excluded. The report further noted that military receipts from the United States were expected to decline by $400 or $500 million in 1956-57 and again in 1957-58, and expressed concern over the long-run outlook for Western Europe's balance of payments because of "the heavy reliance on United States extraordinary expenditures, the failure of exports, particularly dollar exports, to expand with the same rapidity as imports and the difficulties of increasing gold and dollar earnings from third areas" (*Economic Expansion and its Problems*, Paris, February 1956, pp. 51-63). As it turned out, the evolution of U.S. military expenditures abroad was the opposite of that anticipated by the OEEC. From 1954 to 1958 (calendar years) these expenditures rose by $400 million in Western Europe and by an additional $400 million in other areas. In view of the problems presented by German balance-of-payments surpluses, culminating in the upward revaluation of the mark in March 1961, it is ironical to observe that the rise in U.S. military expenditures in Western Europe was entirely attributable to the assumption by the United States of payments for local supplies and services previously furnished by the West German Government. A similar shift in Japan contributed, though in much smaller measure, to the increase noted above in U.S. military expenditures in non-European areas.

[2] Much earlier, in a paper presented shortly after the end of the war, I disagreed with the idea already current of a "chronic" shortage of dollars. While observing that "the position of the United States at the moment seems to be one of unchallenged strength," and that "this lack of balance will be intensified during the next few years until foreign productive capacities are restored," I expressed the view that "it would be foolish to assume that these advantages will remain so unique as they are today," and that "the relationship may be profoundly altered during the next several decades" ("The Domestic Effects of Foreign Investment," *American Economic Review*, May 1946, p. 681).

position were:[3] the high productivity of its mass-production industries; the intensely competitive atmosphere of the United States; its technological and innovational leadership, reposing on large investments in plant and research; the favorable product structure of United States exports of manufactures; the favorable geographic distribution of its exports, with more than half (as against one-tenth for Western Europe) going to the "rapidly growing countries" of the Western Hemisphere; its relative self-sufficiency; United States tariffs on imports of manufactures and its low price elasticity of demand for primary products; its low propensity to invest abroad compared with the strength of its foreign trade position; the supposedly better resistance of the United States to inflationary forces than that shown by other countries; the unlikelihood that American economic aid to other countries would increase enough to fill the gap; the unwillingness of governments to contemplate devaluations on such a scale as would be necessary and the probability that, in any event, the balance would again be disturbed by inflationary tendencies released in the devaluing countries or by the continuation of other adverse trends, and perhaps also by the flight of capital to the United States.

With the pronounced shift in the balance of payments for the worse after 1957, a variety of new explanations have been adduced, some of them the reverse of the propositions previously advanced to explain the dollar shortage. This is not to say that these new explanations do not have great persuasive force and relevance. They do indeed appropriately stress certain basic changes in the world economy which have profoundly affected the international position of the United States; these changes will be examined below in Section 3. One may, however, wonder if there is not again a risk of overexplaining the disequilibrium and of neglecting forces working in the opposite direction; these will also be considered.

[3] The list given is a composite of explanations from various sources. Probably the most uncompromising statement along these lines, though not including all of the elements mentioned, was given as late as April 1957 by Sir Geoffrey Crowther, who referred to his idea conceived twenty years earlier of a "permanent and organic shortage of dollars" and considered that the United States occupied "a position of relative strength without any parallel in economic history" (*Balances and Imbalances of Payments,* Cambridge, Mass., 1957, pp. 34, 45). Sir Donald MacDougall in his major work published about the same time explored the subject in far more detail and with many qualifications but considered that "structural changes" were likely to produce a progressive deterioration in the payments relations of other countries with the United States and saw little hope of a satisfactory solution (*The World Dollar Problem: A Study in International Economics,* London, 1957).

CHART 8

U.S. Payments and Receipts on Basic Transactions in Relation to Gross National Product
(seasonally adjusted, annual rates)

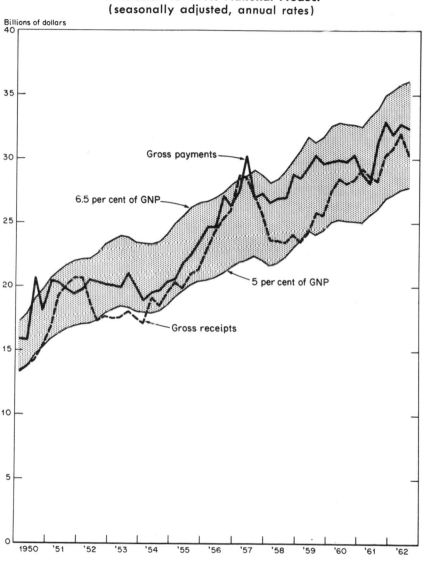

NOTE: Receipts exclude unscheduled debt repayments to U.S. Government.

SOURCE: U.S. Department of Commerce (see also Appendix Tables B-1 and B-2).

The need for caution in developing explanations of balance-of-payments behavior is suggested by the data presented in Chart 8, which shows the gross flows of international receipts and payments of the United States on basic transactions. These flows, though fluctuating enough to produce wide movements in the balance, have adhered to a fairly narrow path in relation to the gross national product. Since 1950, the totals for both gross receipts and gross payments have generally remained within the range of 5 to 6.5 per cent of GNP, payments usually being in the upper part of this band and receipts more often in the lower part.

These comparisons are one way of saying that total foreign transactions and variations in them are small in relation to total American economic activity. They also serve as a reminder that relatively small shifts in the rate at which American incomes are earned or spent abroad may have disturbingly large effects on the balance of payments. The margin to be explained, however crucial in relation to monetary reserves and to the functioning of the economic system, is a fairly narrow one in relation to the sum of economic forces at work.[4]

2. *Increase in Balance-of-Payments Burdens*

The first thing to be noted, before consideration of the more intensive competition facing United States foreign trade, is that the operations to be covered out of the surplus on goods and nonmilitary services have greatly increased during the past decade. It was observed in Chapter I that these operations, net of corresponding receipts, now add up to some $8.5 billion annually. As may be seen in Table 7, this represents an increase of $3 billion over the annual averages during the early 1950's.

By some relevant standards these burdens are not large. They amounted to only 1.7 per cent of gross national product in 1960-1961, and the increase since 1953-1955 is only 2.2 per cent of the increase in gross national product during the same time. They have nevertheless

[4] As Sir Donald MacDougall has said in his reappraisal of the dollar problem: "There is a strong human tendency to assume that the balance of payments cannot change very much from what it is at the moment. This may be due to natural conservatism or perhaps to lack of imagination. In fact it can change very rapidly. The fundamental reason is, I suppose, that it is a marginal part of a marginal part. The balance is a marginal part of the total trade and the trade is in turn a marginal part of the national income" (*The Dollar Problem: A Reappraisal*, Princeton, 1960, p. 64).

TABLE 7

GOVERNMENT TRANSACTIONS[a], PRIVATE INVESTMENT, AND
REMITTANCES AND PENSIONS, BY SELECTED PERIODS, 1950 TO 1962
(millions of dollars, annual averages or annual rates)

	1950-1955	1953-1955	1960-1961	1962, Jan.-Sept.[b]
Payments				
U.S. Government grants and capital	2,912	2,410	3,728	4,303
U.S. military expenditures abroad	2,010	2,719	2,998	2,971
U.S. private long-term investment abroad:				
Direct investment	701	742	1,584	1,239
Portfolio investment	254	125	928	1,092
Remittances and pensions	557	606	860	904
Total	6,433	6,602	10,098	10,509
Receipts				
Repayments on U.S. government loans	406	470	611[c]	599[c]
Receipts by U.S. government on military transactions	192[d]	191	370	916[e]
Foreign long-term investment in U.S.	222	297	448	379
Total	820	958	1,429	1,894
Net payments on foregoing items	5,613	5,644	8,669	8,615
Memorandum items				
Reported U.S. private short-term investment abroad[f]	163	247	1,382	626
Unrecorded payments (errors and omissions)	(345)[g]	(338)[g]	597	696

[a] Excludes ordinary government operations, such as expenditures of the diplomatic service.

[b] Seasonally adjusted; preliminary data.

[c] Excludes unscheduled debt repayments to the U.S. Government (see Tables 1 and A-4).

[d] Includes a rough allowance for receipts from military transactions in 1950-1952 (not separately reported in those years).

[e] Includes deliveries on military sales during the period and $360 million (annual rate) transferred to restricted accounts with the U.S. Treasury on military purchases to be made by foreign countries.

[f] Less changes in foreign commercial credits to the United States.

[g] Net receipts.

SOURCE: U.S. Department of Commerce.

imposed the need for a much faster rate of growth in exports than in imports, not merely an increase sufficient to close the deficit on basic transactions which had already developed. If, for instance, imports of goods and nonmilitary services had risen by 50 per cent from the 1953-1955 level—or slightly less than the actual increase to the first half of 1962—exports of goods and nonmilitary services would have needed to increase by about 65 per cent, the relevant computations being as follows (in millions of dollars):

Assume an increase of 50 per cent in imports of goods and nonmilitary services from the 1953-1955 annual average of 14,000 (Table 14)	7,000
Add: actual increase to first nine months of 1962 in annual rate of net government expenditures abroad, private long-term investments, and remittances and pensions (Table 7)	3,000
Add: deficit on basic transactions in 1953-1955, annual average (Table 6)	1,700
Equals: additional exports of goods and nonmilitary services needed over 1953-1955 annual average of 18,000; that is, an increase of 65 per cent	11,700

Because exports of goods and nonmilitary services in 1953-1955 were already so much larger than corresponding imports, a 50 per cent increase in both would have sufficed to eliminate the deficit on basic transactions in the absence of a rise in the expenditures listed in Table 7. But, with the increase in these expenditures, an appreciably faster rate of growth in exports has been needed—a need only partially fulfilled so far, as will be discussed in Section 4 of this chapter.

If it were considered also necessary to cover, rather than curb, outflows of liquid capital on the scale experienced in 1960-1961, the required increase in exports of goods and nonmilitary services over the 1953-1955 level, under the conditions stated above, would have been more than 75 per cent (the additional amount being the net change of $2,070 million in the memorandum items given at the bottom of Table 7).[5] In absolute amount, the increase needed in exports ($13,800 million) would have been almost twice as great as that

---

[5] In this computation it is assumed that the shift in unrecorded transactions can be attributed to movements of liquid capital. See pp. 16-17.

assumed in imports of goods and nonmilitary services.[6]

It may be useful to stress again a point mentioned in Chapter I, namely, that the various expenditures abroad listed in Table 7 and the trade surplus are not independent of each other. Thus, the greater part by far of government grants and credits is directly spent on United States goods and services, including deliveries of farm products under our surplus disposal programs.[7] This is also true of a part, albeit a smaller part, of our private investments abroad insofar as disbursements are made for the procurement of equipment and materials in the United States. To the extent that this is so, it may ease the "transfer problem" —that is, the problem of developing an export surplus to compensate for the rise in government expenditures and private investment abroad.[8] It is possible, however, to exaggerate the extent of the relief afforded by a deliberate policy of tying foreign economic aid to purchases here: if the beneficiary countries' high-priority demands for United States goods are financed in this way, they then have greater leeway to apply their own foreign exchange earnings to the satisfaction of their demands on other sources of supply. In other words, the net effect on the United States balance of payments is not necessarily different in all cases when economic aid is tied and when it is not.[9] In any event, it seems clear that the greater part of the net figure of $8.6 billion shown in Table 7

[6] This puts the problem in an extreme form, but, as further noted subsequently, something would need to be allowed for the exports made possible by short-term credits extended by this country.

[7] See Chart 1. The funds may also be used in part to refinance outstanding obligations to the United States.

[8] The "transfer problem" was the subject in 1929 of a lively controversy between Keynes and Bertil Ohlin in the *Economic Journal* with regard to Germany's ability to pay reparations growing out of the First World War. Their articles, along with a 1942 commentary by Lloyd A. Metzler, are reprinted in *Readings in the Theory of International Trade*, Philadelphia, 1950. In connection with the policy of tying U.S. government expenditures to procurement in the United States, it is interesting to recall Ohlin's concluding comment: "In principle, the safest and simplest way of organising the reparation payments would be a policy of deliveries in kind from Germany to France and the South American nations, which require imports of many commodities German industry is well able to produce." Ohlin foresaw as a major obstacle, however, "the inevitable opposition of powerful American and British export industries" (*ibid.*, p. 178).

[9] For a discussion of some of these complex relations, see *Survey of Current Business*, September 1961, pp. 9-12, and June 1962, pp. 15-24.

accrues to other countries as part of their freely usable foreign exchange resources and is employed in accordance with the dictates of market and other forces. The United States has therefore needed to strengthen its competitive position to accommodate these payments.

3. *Factors of Change in Our Competitive Position*

GROWTH OF FOREIGN CAPACITY AND ELIMINATION OF BOTTLENECKS

At the same time that our financial commitments were rising over the past decade, some important supports to our export surplus were falling away. The swift growth of production in Europe and Japan, along with the reduction in excess purchasing power through monetary reform and price increases, brought supply and demand into better balance in these countries, making them less dependent on the United States as a source of supply and increasingly able to compete with it.

These changes bore more heavily on some parts of our trade than on others, and it may be useful to note some of their specific effects on products of considerable prominence in our exports. Thus, for some years after the war, energy was a bottleneck abroad. Coal was in short supply, the construction of oil refineries was only beginning, and electric power generating capacity had fallen far behind demand. As another example, Europe had lagged badly behind the United States in the development of continuous strip mills, and sheet steel production was until very recently inadequate to meet the needs of the booming automobile industry. These conditions created heavy demands on the United States in Europe and Japan, and also in third markets, for fuels and industrial materials as well as for capital equipment for their production. One by one these shortages disappeared, and with them the exceptional support which they had provided to United States exports.[10]

INCREASED RECEPTIVITY OF THE UNITED STATES TO IMPORTS

Still another major change affecting our trade and payments position is that the United States is much more open to foreign competition today than at any time in recent decades. Sir Donald MacDougall has

[10] In this connection, note especially the behavior of the items in Group I of Table 2 and the discussion on p. 30.

pointed out that, for a succession of reasons, the United States was largely sheltered from imports of manufactures over most of the last thirty years or more.[11] The inhibiting factors included our high tariffs of the interwar period, the stultifying effects of the depression in the 1930's, the disruption of normal trade during the war years, the early postwar shortages in other countries, and the time they required to rebuild export outlets.

Now, for the first time in many years, other manufacturing countries have both the possibility and the incentive to compete in the American market. Our import duties are much lower over a broad range of goods, both because of actual reductions in rates of duty from those set in the 1930 tariff and because the rise in prices since then has diminished the effect of specific duties. Our merchants have become active in seeking out foreign suppliers, even to the extent of initiating production and providing technical help, and foreign styling and a foreign label have a wider appeal to customers than before. In these circumstances the selling drives launched by foreign countries in the days of the dollar shortage are bearing fruit.

The recent rapid growth of United States imports of manufactures may therefore represent the concentration in a few years of a development that, without the inhibiting circumstances mentioned, might well have stretched out over several decades and permitted more leisurely adjustment in our trade and payments.

FOREIGN TECHNOLOGICAL ADVANCE

Many of our manufactures, even if sometimes costly, sell on the basis of the advanced technology which they embody. A few years ago a Danish economist, Erik Hoffmeyer, developed the thesis that United States imports consisted mainly of traditional commodities, while its exports consisted increasingly of new and research-intensive products.[12] These included, in particular, machinery and vehicles, chemicals, synthetic fibers, scientific and professional instruments, and photographic goods. Hoffmeyer's recapitulation of our export statistics showed that the share of these groups in our total exports had increased from 12 per cent just before the First World War to 24 per cent in the late 1920's and to 44 per cent in 1953-54.

[11] *The Dollar Problem: A Reappraisal,* pp. 41-42.

[12] *Dollar Shortage and the Structure of U.S. Foreign Trade,* Copenhagen and Amsterdam, 1958.

As noted earlier in this chapter, this characteristic of our exports figured prominently in the expectation widely held only a few years ago that the rest of the world was likely to face continuing difficulty in balancing accounts with the United States. Even if our production costs were high, it was said, other countries were bound to be avid customers for the latest products of our advanced technology. Some of these would eventually be put into production abroad, but meanwhile the United States would enjoy a lead in their sale and would be developing other more advanced products to take their place. Nowadays, this argument is used in reverse to explain the present oversupply of dollars.[13] Other countries, it is said, have also been making rapid strides in their technology and, in a general climate of growth and innovation, are reducing our leadtime in industrial application. This process is aided by the growth of United States manufacturing and licensing operations abroad which incorporate our latest technology, and many American companies are now also engaging in original research and development activity in other countries.

In this view, therefore, the competitive conditions in world trade have drastically altered, with effects on both our exports and our imports, and the United States must increasingly be prepared to compete on a price basis and to make whatever adjustments in its cost and price levels may be necessary to this end.

While recognizing the technological strides being made by our competitors, one may ask if there is not some risk of underrating our own progress. Expenditures on research and development in the United States are estimated to have doubled in real terms, or trebled in money terms, from 1953 to 1961 to a total of approximately $15 billion, or one-third as much as business expenditures on fixed capital. Though more than 55 per cent of the total is accounted for by the aircraft and parts industry and the electrical equipment and communications industry, indicative of the role of defense contracts, research and development outlays have been increasing rapidly in other industries as well.[14] It

---

[13] Cf., for example, Charles P. Kindleberger, "United States Economic Foreign Policy: Research Requirements for 1965," *World Politics*, July 1959, and Albert O. Hirschman, "Invitation to Theorizing About the Dollar Glut," *The Review of Economics and Statistics*, February 1960.

[14] *Economic Report of the President*, January 1962, pp. 123-127 (based on statistics compiled by the National Science Foundation). See also National Science Foundation, *Funds For Research and Development in Industry, 1957, 1958, 1959*, Washington, 1960, 1961, 1962, pp. 73, 51, and 53, respectively.

seems likely that the part devoted primarily to defense purposes may also yield a significant return in technological progress of civilian application.[15]

A recent British study undertook to compare the amount of expenditure on research and development performed by industry, including that financed by the government, in the United States and the United Kingdom in 1959, and summed up its findings as follows:

> After adjusting the exchange rate to get a comparison which is, as near as possible, in real terms, it seems that American industry's research expenditure is over five times as large as British industry's, as an absolute figure; it is nearly three times as large per employee, and twice as large as a percentage of net output. Taking the 350 largest firms in each country which do research, the average large American firm spends five times as much as the average large British one.[16]

Though these data on the increase and relative size of research and development expenditures in the United States are reassuring as far as they go, they need to be supplemented by more thorough investigation into the factors bearing on our competitive position in technologically advanced products. It may be, for instance, that industrial research efforts in the United States are unduly focused on getting quick market results, in contrast to basic research leading to new

[15] A skeptical view on this subject is expressed in *The Nation's Engineering Research Needs 1965-1985*, Summary Report of the Engineering Research Committee, Engineers Joint Council, May 25, 1962. In its conclusions the report expresses the view that "The present system for allocating resources to U.S. research and development programs is producing an apparent imbalance in our technical effort, with emphasis on defense-atomic-space activities and on the rapid exploitation of new scientific developments, with an accompanying relatively complete neglect of basic need-oriented engineering programs." It further states that "the nondefense agencies of the Federal government do not have adequate research programs," and that "industries which have little contact with defense programs tend to provide minimal support for research and development, suggesting that they are not able to compete with Federal research and development programs, or that they are organized in such a way that they cannot undertake research and development as it is performed today."

[16] "Research and Development: A Comparison Between British and American Industry," *Economic Review* (London, National Institute of Economic and Social Research), May 1962, pp. 21-39. It may be noted that the study employs a "research" exchange rate of $6.30 to the pound (compared with the official rate of $2.80), reflecting chiefly the much higher level of salaries of scientists and engineers in the United States. Costs of materials, according to the study, "are not much—if at all—more expensive in the United States."

scientific discoveries and technological innovations.[17] At the same time one may ask if the role of research as an independent economic factor may not be overstated in relation to other influences, such as growth of incomes and markets, contributing to the development of modern large-scale industry in other countries and to the increase in their competitive power in "research-intensive" products.[18]

PRICES AND COMPETITION

In its most general formulation, the judgment that United States prices are too high does not rely on statistical evidence of differences in prices or price movements at home and abroad but only on the fact of the deficit itself. By this test—whatever the relative magnitude of past inflation indicated by international comparisons extending back to some base period—United States prices are at a level higher than would be compatible with the growth in its foreign commitments and the increase in the productive power and financial discipline of its competitors.[19]

It is important but difficult to proceed beyond this very broad statement and to form a judgment as to how serious the disparity between United States and foreign prices may be. Actual export price quotations from both home and foreign sources are few and difficult

[17] This criticism is strongly expressed in a paper, "The Role of Research and Engineering Effectiveness in World Chemical Competition," presented by P. W. Blaylock on December 7, 1961, at the Annual Meeting of the American Institute of Chemical Engineers. Mr. Blaylock contrasted the "commercially oriented company" and the "scientifically oriented company," and complained that "the money reported as having been spent on 'research' is no measure of the fruitfulness of the work which was done. . . . Vast sums are spent on 'modifying, refining, testing and perfecting' other peoples' inventions as soon as they have become fashionable. All goes well until the supply of these inventions runs short. Then profits suffer and the basic weakness of the commercially oriented firm is exposed." In his conclusions Mr. Blaylock said: "We learned that an organization which can manufacture and sell with great efficiency can, nevertheless, be intellectually sterile. Finally, we saw that an increase in the amount of money spent on research and an increase in the number of scientists employed will not ensure an increased flow of inventions. Small, modest groups of scientists can turn out a creditable flow of inventions if they work in the right environment. It is the North American corporate climate which is at fault. This is what must be corrected if we are to improve the efficiency of our research in the future."

[18] Cf. Irving Kravis, " 'Availability' and Other Influences on the Commodity Composition of Trade," *Journal of Political Economy,* April 1956.

[19] Cf. Gottfried Haberler, "Domestic Economic Policies and the United States Balance of Payments," in Seymour E. Harris (ed.), *The Dollar in Crisis,* New York, 1961, pp. 63-65.

to compare, especially for the highly fabricated and differentiated products in which we are most interested. It is hoped that information in this vital area will be greatly improved by the intensive investigation into comparative prices and related factors in the United States and abroad which the National Bureau has undertaken.[20]

More information is available on relative price changes as measured by the various price indexes compiled in each country. We may therefore hope to get at least some idea of how far prices have altered to our disadvantage during, say, the past decade, even though we still lack any solid basis for judging our comparative price position at any point of time. Tables 8 and 9 give national wholesale and consumer price indexes and the implicit price deflators of gross national products for a number of countries. These indexes are, however, subject to serious shortcomings because of differences in composition and methodology, and they are heavily weighted with products which do not enter foreign trade. The latter difficulty is obviated by the so-called "unit value" indexes given in Table 10 for United States exports and imports and in Table 11 for exports of manufactures by the United States and other industrial countries. Such "unit value" indexes suffer, however, from other grave deficiencies. They either cover only a small and not necessarily representative part of trade in manufactured goods or contain heterogeneous commodity aggregates for which changes in unit values may reflect shifts in composition or quality rather than price changes.[21]

Because of the deficiencies in these various measures, they do not lend themselves to firm conclusions about the relative course of United States and foreign prices. The rise after 1953 in the general level of prices does not appear to have been markedly greater, if at all, in the United States than in most other leading industrial countries.[22]

[20] See the Preface to this paper for further comments on the new project.

[21] For a critical appraisal of "unit value" indexes, see *The Price Statistics of the Federal Government*, New York, NBER, 1961, pp. 79-86, and Robert E. Lipsey, *Price and Quantity Trends in the Foreign Trade of the United States* (in press).

[22] This conclusion seems to emerge clearly from the implicit price deflators in Table 9 for total gross national product and for personal consumption, and to be supported also by the movements of the consumer price indexes in Table 8. The wholesale price index, on the other hand, rose more, especially up to about 1959 or 1960, in the United States than in other industrial countries, the United Kingdom and Sweden being important exceptions (and France also except as offset by devaluation of the franc).

TABLE 8

Indexes of Wholesale and Consumer Prices, U.S. and
Other Industrial Countries
(1953 = 100)

		1957	1958	1959	1960	1961	1962 October
United States							
Wholesale prices	A	106.8	108.3	108.4	108.6	108.2	108.6
Consumer prices	A	105.0	107.9	108.9	110.6	111.8	113.7
Belgium							
Wholesale prices	A	106.3	101.7	101.3	102.6	102.4	101.7a
Consumer prices	A	106.9	108.3	109.6	110.0	111.1	112.7
France							
Wholesale prices	A	108.2	120.7	126.5	129.7	132.4	135.1
	B	103.0	100.5	89.7	92.0	93.9	95.8
Consumer prices	A	105.5	121.5	128.9	133.6	137.2	145.7
	B	100.5	101.2	91.4	94.8	97.3	103.4
Germany, Fed. Rep.							
Wholesale prices	A B	} 103.4	103.0	102.2	103.4	{ 104.9 109.3	106.3 111.6
Consumer prices	A B	} 106.6	108.8	109.9	111.5	{ 114.3 119.1	118.1 124.3
Italy							
Wholesale prices	A	102.7	100.9	97.9	98.8	99.0	102.2a
Consumer prices	A	110.2	113.3	112.8	115.4	117.8	124.2a
Japan							
Wholesale prices	A	105	98	99	101	105	105
Consumer prices	A	109	109	110	114	120	129
Netherlands							
Wholesale prices	A B	} 107.4	105.2	105.8	103.2	{ 102.5 106.8	102b 107b
Consumer prices	A B	} 115	117	118	121	{ 123 128	128a 135a
Sweden							
Wholesale prices	A	110	107	107	111	113	115a
Consumer prices	A	113	119	120	124	127	134
Switzerland							
Wholesale prices	A	105.1	101.8	100.2	100.8	101.0	104.1
Consumer prices	A	105.1	107.2	106.4	107.9	110.0	115.5
United Kingdom							
Wholesale prices	A	110.7	111.4	111.8	113.3	116.3	119.4
Consumer prices	A	115.8	119.3	120.0	121.2	125.3	130.4

NOTES TO TABLE 8

A = Indexes of price changes in national currencies.

B = Indexes of price changes expressed in dollars where exchange parities have altered.

a September.

b August.

SOURCE: Japan, United Nations, *Monthly Bulletin of Statistics*, July 1961, p. 144, and December 1962, pp. 120-121 and 144-145; other countries, OECD Statistical Bulletins, *Main Economic Indicators*, November 1962, p. 12.

This generalization does not hold, however, for capital goods and related items which are of crucial importance in United States foreign trade. In particular, prices of machinery and steel appear to have risen much more here than in Europe during the 1955-1959 period, as reflected in the price deflators for machinery and equipment in Table 9.

Our unfavorable position in steel appears to be borne out by other data[23] and by the course of trade. In machinery, the significance of the comparison is less clear because of differences in types and qualities and because of the strength of our export performance. This strength could mean that the rapid growth of the economies of Western Europe and Japan in recent years has generated a good demand for our machinery, despite the apparently greater increase in United States prices for these products. One would also need to allow, however, for the possibility that the divergencies in reported price trends reflect not only differences in supply prices for the same products but also differences in demand for different products. If, for instance, American production and exports of machinery are more heavily weighted than production and exports of other countries with products of advanced technology for which world demand has been particularly strong, the relatively greater increase in United States price indexes, so weighted, would not necessarily measure a deterioration in its competitive position.

Since about 1959, there seems to have been no further increase, and perhaps rather some decrease, in United States prices compared

[23] On the basis of unweighted averages of indexes of four types of steel (bars, plates, sheets, and structurals) given in a study by Hang Sheng Cheng, steel prices increased 20 per cent from 1953-1957 both in the United States and in the European Coal and Steel Community, and then rose by a further 5 percentage points to 1959 in the United States but fell by some 20 per cent in the ECSC ("Relative Movements in the Prices of Exports of Manufactures: United States Versus Other Industrial Countries, 1953-59," IMF *Staff Papers*, March 1962, p. 80).

TABLE 9

IMPLICIT PRICE DEFLATORS FOR GROSS NATIONAL PRODUCT AND
SELECTED COMPONENTS, UNITED STATES AND EUROPEAN MEMBERS OF OECD
(1953 = 100)

		1955	1957	1959	1960	1961
Gross national product, total						
United States	A	102	109	114	115	117
OECD, excl. U.S. and Canada[a]	B	104	111	110	113	118
Belgium	A	102	111	112	114	115p
France	A B	} 102	{ 113 { 106	134 96	139 99	144 103
Germany, Fed. Rep.	A B	} 102	109	115	118	{ 123 { 129
Italy	A	104	109	111	113	115
Netherlands	A B	} 108	119	122	124	{ 126 { 132
Sweden	A	104	113	118	123	126
United Kingdom	A	106	116	121	123	127
Capital formation, total						
United States	A	103	115	118	120	120
OECD, excl. U.S. and Canada[a]	B	102	110	108	110	115
Belgium	A	103	115	116	118	118p
France	A B	} 101	{ 113 { 105	127 91	130 93	133 95
Germany, Fed. Rep.	A B	} 102	109	113	118	{ 124 { 129
Italy	A	102	108	107	108	111
Netherlands	A B	} 107	122	123	124	{ 125 { 131
Sweden	A	102	111	112	119	123
United Kingdom	A	105	114	116	116	119

(continued)

TABLE 9 (concluded)

		1955	1957	1959	1960	1961
Capital formation: machinery and equipment						
United States	A	104	117	122	123	122
OECD, excl. U.S. and Canada[a]	B	101	107	105	106	110
Belgium	A	102	113	113	115	115p
France	A B	} 99	{ 107 { 100	123 88	127 90	130 93
Germany, Fed. Rep.	A B	} 98	105	105	107	{ 110 { 115
Italy	A	98	103	100	100	102
Netherlands	A B	} 100	110	109	110	{ 110 { 115
Sweden	A	98	109	109	116	119
United Kingdom	A	104	115	118	118	122
Personal consumption, total						
United States	A	101	106	110	111	112
OECD, excl. U.S. and Canada[a]	B	104	109	107	110	113
Belgium	A	102	108	109	109	110p
France	A B	} 103	{ 113 { 105	133 95	138 98	143 102
Germany, Fed. Rep.	A B	} 103	108	112	114	{ 117 { 122
Italy	A	104	109	110	111	112
Netherlands	A B	} 106	113	116	118	{ 120 { 126
Sweden	A	104	112	116	120	123
United Kingdom	A	100	114	118	119	122

A = Indexes of price changes in national currencies.
B = Indexes of price changes expressed in dollars where exchange parities have altered.

[a] Includes, in addition to European countries listed, Luxembourg, Austria, Denmark, Greece, Iceland, Ireland, Norway, Switzerland, Portugal, and Turkey.
p Preliminary estimate.
SOURCE: From data supplied by the OECD.

TABLE 10

U.S. EXPORT AND IMPORT "UNIT VALUE" INDEXES AND EXPORT-WEIGHTED INDEXES DERIVED FROM COMPONENTS OF WHOLESALE PRICE INDEX

	Average Value of Exports or Imports 1957-1959 (millions of dollars)	Index Numbers (1953 = 100)[a]				1962	
		1955	1957	1959	1961	First Quarter	Second Quarter
"Unit value" indexes							
Exports, total[b]	18,628	100.0	106.4	106.4	109.6	111.7	109.6
Finished manufactures	11,101	100.0	110.1	114.6	120.2	122.5	121.3
Semimanufactures	2,671	106.5	115.2	105.4	104.3	104.3	101.1
Finished manufactures and semimanufactures[c]	13,773	101.3	111.1	112.8	117.1	119.0	117.4
Imports, total[b]	13,948	102.0	105.1	99.0	99.0	97.0	97.0
Finished manufactures	4,204	99.0	102.0	100.0	103.0	101.0	102.0
Semimanufactures	2,962	105.2	109.3	100.0	101.0	97.9	96.9
Finished manufactures and semimanufactures[c]	7,166	101.6	105.0	100.0	102.2	99.7	99.9
Export-weighted indexes derived from WPI components[d]							
1. Machinery and vehicles	6,540	104.4	118.9	124.3	124.5	124.5	124.4
2. Metals and manufactures	1,751	107.7	119.3	121.1	120.5	120.3	119.8
3. Chemicals and related products	1,424	100.8	103.6	104.1	103.1	102.1	101.7
4. Sawmill products and wood manufactures	133	102.9	99.1	104.7	96.5	95.9	97.7
5. Pulp and paper products	322	102.7	111.6	113.9	111.4	113.0	113.7
6. Rubber and manufactures	304	114.9	116.1	115.5	111.4	108.7	107.8

(continued)

TABLE 10 (concluded)

	Average Value of Exports or Imports 1957-1959 (millions of dollars)	Index Numbers (1953 = 100)[a]				1962	
		1955	1957	1959	1961	First Quarter	Second Quarter
7. Textile semimanufactures and finished manufactures	634	98.0	98.1	97.7	97.0	97.7	97.9
8. Petroleum and products	677	99.4	112.5	102.0	105.0	103.1	103.9
9. Coal and related products	589	92.9	110.3	108.6	106.8	107.9	103.7
10. Manufactured foodstuffs	1,114	97.2	100.9	102.3	103.7	104.8	102.9
11. Crude foodstuffs and other agricultural materials	2,926	92.4	93.7	91.8	90.7	92.7	90.8
12. Miscellaneous products (mainly manufactures)	1,185	94.0	91.7	96.7	98.6	100.2	100.6
Total, all groups (1 to 12)	17,599	100.6	108.9	110.9	110.7	111.1	110.4
Total, excluding miscellaneous (1 to 11)	16,414	101.1	110.2	111.9	111.6	111.8	111.2
Manufactures, including miscellaneous products (1 to 7 + 12)	12,293	103.3	113.0	116.8	116.6	116.6	116.5
Manufactures, excluding miscellaneous products (1 to 7)	11,108	104.3	115.3	118.9	118.5	118.4	118.2

NOTES TO TABLE 10

a Converted from 1957-1959 base as published in sources indicated.

b "Unit value" indexes for total exports and total imports include (in addition to finished manufactures and semimanufactures) crude materials, crude foodstuffs, and manufactured foodstuffs.

c The separate indexes for "finished manufactures" and semimanufactures" are combined (according to their weights as given in the first column) for closer, but still imperfect, comparability with the series for exports of "manufactures" as defined in Table 11.

d Indexes given in the last four lines of the table have been obtained by applying weights derived from the export values shown in the first column to the following groups or subgroups of the wholesale price index, numbered as in the stub: (1) machinery and motive products; (2) metals and metal products; (3) chemicals and allied products; (4) lumber and wood products; (5) pulp, paper, and allied products; (6) rubber and products; (7) textile products and apparel; (8) petroleum products, refined; (9) coal; (10) processed foods; (11) farm products; (12) miscellaneous.

SOURCE: U.S. Department of Commerce and Bureau of Labor Statistics.

with those of most other countries. The further increase since 1959 in the United States "unit value" index for exports of manufactures is, however, puzzling. Though little or no greater than in the corresponding series in Table 11 for other industrial countries except Italy and Japan, this increase appears out of line with the behavior of both the United States wholesale price index and the price deflator for machinery and equipment. This difference in movement has prompted the construction of crude export-weighted indexes derived from components of the United States domestic wholesale price index in the manner indicated in the lower part of Table 10. The indexes shown for manufactures (last two lines of the table) conform fairly well to the general movement shown by the "unit value" series for manufactures up to 1959, but exhibit marked stability since then in contrast to the continued rise in the export "unit value" series—a divergence which, on the surface, appears implausible in view of the intensified competition which has developed in international trade. Here again, more detailed research is needed, but this comparison would appear to cast doubt on the reliability and international comparability of the "unit

TABLE 11

"Unit Value" Indexes of Exports of Manufactures,
United States and Other Industrial Countries[a]
(1953 = 100)

	1955	1957	1959	1960	1961	1962 Jan.-Sept.
United States	101	112	116	118	121	122[b]
Belgium-Luxembourg	96	102	95	95	95	95[b]
France	100	104	94	99	100	99[b]
Germany, Fed. Rep.	96	101	99	100	105	107
Italy	92	90	80	83	80	n.a.
Japan	91	97	93	94	91	89
Netherlands	98	103	101	101	105	n.a.
Sweden	100	107	108	110	113	112
United Kingdom	101	108	110	113	114	115

[a] National series converted to dollar equivalent where exchange rates have altered. "Manufactures" comprise, in principle, Sections 5 to 8 of the Standard International Trade Classification and differ to some extent in coverage from any of the series given in Table 10.

[b] January-June.

Source: Statistical Office of the United Nations.

value" indexes in Table 11.[24]

Perhaps more important than price indexes as a guide to the future, there is evidence that our cost position vis-à-vis other countries

[24] These questions are of some importance, given a common tendency to pay homage to the imperfections of the "unit value" series and then nevertheless to draw conclusions from them. It must be remembered that the "price" data for these indexes are derived by dividing (where both are available) reported values by reported quantities for individual items in the trade statistics. Even though great care may be exercised in the selection of items, as in the computation of the U.S. series, one may doubt that a representative sample can be obtained in this way, especially with regard to highly developed manufactures for which significant physical measures are usually lacking. These doubts apply, of course, not only to the U.S. indexes but also to those for other countries.

has also improved over this period. In the United States labor costs per unit of output in manufacturing seem to be no higher, on the average, than in 1957, the increase in hourly earnings being offset by the rise in output per manhour. For some of our leading competitors, on the other hand, the labor market has become very tight, especially for skilled workers, and, as may be seen in Table 12, labor costs per unit of output are tending to rise.[25]

In Western Germany, perhaps the most important case in point, productivity gains are no longer outdistancing wage increases. From the second quarter of 1960 to the second quarter of 1962, hourly earnings in German industry rose by almost one-fourth, or more than two and a half times as much as the rise in output per manhour over this period.[26] If we also take account of the 5 per cent revaluation of the mark in March 1961, wage costs per unit of output in German manufacturing were about 20 per cent higher, in dollar terms, in mid-1962 than two years earlier. Even if German producers absorb the difference, these increases should do something to shift the relative attractions of the internal and external markets and to adjust the balance of trade. Complaints about the profits squeeze in the United States now have a familiar echo in Germany and other Western European countries.

It seems likely that these upward pressures on European labor costs will continue. Additions to the labor force will be smaller in some countries for demographic reasons, and potentially large transfers out of agriculture may be inhibited by the high prices to be paid to farmers under the policies agreed upon by the Common Market. Having already become accustomed to high annual wage increases, European labor is in a strong position, under these conditions, to press its objectives, including that of shorter hours with no reduction in pay. Within the

[25] Different results are obtained for the United States, especially in computing the change in labor costs from 1953 to 1957, depending on whether manufacturing output is measured by the Federal Reserve index of production or by the Bureau of Labor Statistics series on net output in manufacturing. (For a summary discussion of the differences between these series see the *Survey of Current Business*, October 1962, pp. 17, 18.) This difference in results is indicative of the problems encountered in measuring unit labor costs in any one country and of the uncertainty attaching to international comparisons of the results for different countries.

[26] The increase in hourly earnings refers to all German industry, that in output per manhour to manufacturing industry only. See *Economic Review* (National Institute of Economic and Social Research, London), November 1962, Table 22, p. 59.

TABLE 12

PERCENTAGE CHANGE IN LABOR COST PER UNIT OF OUTPUT IN MANUFACTURING IN THE UNITED STATES AND OTHER LEADING INDUSTRIAL COUNTRIES, 1953 TO 1957 AND 1957 TO 1961

Line	Country	1953 to 1957 Output per Manhour or per Man(*) (1)	Labor Cost per Hour or per Man(*) (2)	Labor Cost per Unit of Output[a] (3)	1957 to 1961 Output per Manhour or per Man(*) (4)	Labor Cost per Hour or per Man(*) (5)	Labor Cost per Unit of Output[a] (6)
	All Employees						
	United States, with output measured by:						
1.	BLS index	7	22	13	14	16	2
2.	FRB index	13	22	8	15	16	1
3.	France	40	52	{ 9 / 1[b]	26	37[c]	{ 9 / —15[b]
4.	Japan	31	22	—7	35	30	—3
5.	Netherlands	15*	50	30	20*	19	{ —1 / 4[d]
6.	United Kingdom	10*e	31*	18	10*e	24*	13
	Production Workers						
	United States, with output measured by:						
7.	BLS index	13	20	6	18	14	—4
8.	FRB index	18	20	2	19	14	—4
9.	Germany, Fed. Rep.	24	34	8	28	41	{ 10 / 15[d]
10.	Italy	30*	24	—5	22*	19[c]	—2
11.	Sweden	13*	31	—16	15*	28	11
12.	United Kingdom	13*	31*	16	13*	23*	9

NOTES TO TABLE 12

SOURCE: For all except lines 2, 6, 8, and 12: Computed by the Bureau of Labor Statistics, Department of Labor, from sources indicated in Tables C-3 and C-4 of the paper "Foreign Trade and Collective Bargaining" delivered by Philip Arnow, Assistant Commissioner of Labor Statistics, to the Industrial Relations Research Association, Detroit, May 1960. The Bureau of Labor Statistics notes that it is not in a position to determine the comparability or reliability of the basic statistics from which these unit-labor cost indexes were derived. The calculations should be regarded as tentative estimates which have required various assumptions or projections and which may therefore be subject to error. Adjustments have been made by the BLS to include wage supplements in the labor cost data given in columns 2 and 5.

Lines 2 and 8: NBER computation, employing Federal Reserve index of manufacturing production instead of Bureau of Labor Statistics index of net output in manufacturing to derive entries for columns 1, 3, 4, and 6.

Lines 6 and 12: NBER computation based on data given on manufacturing output, number of wage earners and salary earners employed in manufacturing, and total wage bill and salary bill in manufacturing in Tables 14 and 17 of *National Income and Expenditure 1962*, London.

a Where output is given per man (*) and labor cost per manhour, the assumption is made that the latter moved in the same way as labor cost per man (i.e., that there has been no change in hours worked).

b Equivalent in dollar terms, reflecting devaluation of the French franc by approximately 16.7 per cent in August 1957 and by a further 15 per cent in December 1958.

c Preliminary.

d Equivalent in dollar terms, reflecting upward revaluation of the German and Dutch currencies by 5 per cent in March 1961.

e According to an index published by the National Institute of Economic and Social Research, London, output *per manhour* worked by all employees in manufacturing rose by 9 per cent from 1953 to 1957 and by 13 per cent from 1957 to 1961 (*Economic Review*, November 1962, Table 8, p. 52).

Common Market there is also strong pressure, especially from France, for equal pay for women, now substantially lower than men's wages in other countries of the group.

AMERICAN INVESTMENT IN FOREIGN MANUFACTURING

The growth of American foreign investment, or more specifically that part of it going into manufacturing operations in Western Europe, deserves further attention with respect to both its implications and its consequences for the international competitive position of the United States.

Apart from the present and future effects of these investments on the balance of payments, they are sometimes looked upon as evidence in themselves of differences in production costs between the United States and other countries. On this view, the rapid swelling of American manufacturing operations in Western Europe during the last several years is in itself an indication of weakness in our competitive position vis-à-vis other industrial countries.

One cannot but be impressed by the breadth and strength of this development of foreign operations by American companies. What it signifies for our competitiveness, however, is not clear. Comparative advantage never lies wholly on one side or the other, else there would be no basis for international trade. It seems plausible to assume that, in the absence of any special deterrents, American firms would be actively investing abroad. It is also evident, however, that until quite recently conditions over most of the last three decades were not such as to encourage American investment in Europe. One has only to recall the economic and monetary disturbances associated with the Great Depression of the early 1930's, the growing political and military tensions as the war approached, five years of active warfare in Europe, and then the early postwar years of shortages and controls and still several years more until, at the end of 1958, European currencies were once again convertible. World political uncertainty is perhaps greater than ever, and yet, here too, the development of nuclear weapons tends to equalize military risks and to remove whatever preference the United States may have enjoyed in relative security. Perhaps, then, American companies are now crowding into a few hurried years the expansion of their foreign manufacturing operations which, under more propitious conditions, they would have developed over the last several decades.

This concentration, or catching up, of investment activity is true in a larger sense of the impressive growth of the Western European economy in general during the past ten years. This adds to the inducement to American firms, especially those having large funds to invest and limited incentive to spend them on expanding capacity in the more slowly growing American economy. Without minimizing the contribution which economic policies on one side and the other may have made to this disparity in growth rates, a considerable part of it, perhaps the greater part, may be simply attributable to the earlier failure in Europe, under prewar and wartime conditions, to develop industries which in America had already reached high levels of capacity and technology. The rapid postwar development of automobile production and transportation in Europe must alone have provided a powerful stimulus to the development of other industries, especially steel, petroleum refining, and highway construction, as well as a host of ancillary manufacturing and service industries in each case.

In this atmosphere of growth in Europe, the Common Market has developed a mystique of its own, coupled with the more tangible attraction to production within the area provided by a common external tariff on imports from outside and the progressive elimination of duties on trade among the members. The inducement to American firms to establish operations abroad, and to reinvest earnings in the further expansion of capacity, may also have been enhanced by lower taxes than in this country, especially when the amount of taxes effectively paid could be reduced by channeling sales and other receipts of foreign subsidiaries to one of the "tax haven" countries.[27] The possibilities of

[27] In most European countries the income tax rates to which American manufacturing companies are subject appear to be only moderately lower than in the United States. Thus, the Department of Commerce, after noting that in the fiscal year 1957 manufacturing enterprises in the United States paid about 48 per cent of their income in income taxes, gave the following percentages as having been paid by U.S. direct-investment enterprises in Europe on the basis of data reported in the Department's census of foreign investments (*U.S. Business Investments in Foreign Countries,* Washington, 1960, p. 46): Belgium, 27; France, 52; Germany, 40; Italy, 40; Netherlands, 43; United Kingdom, 45. The rates paid may have been of only nominal significance, however, insofar as profits could be shifted from the country of production to Switzerland or some other "tax haven" country. The motivations on the part of the host country in consenting to arrangements entailing such a loss of revenue were discussed in an interpellation in the Dutch Parliament, reported as follows in a study of taxes in relation to foreign investments in the Common Market countries:

"The Common Market countries recognize that this practice of effecting sales through Swiss base companies is being followed. In this connection the Minister of Finance of the Netherlands was reminded in the legislature that, 'as a matter of fact, some big groups are establishing factories in our country, but, besides, have founded sales companies in Switzerland. Obviously, therefore, they wish to take advantage of the cheap rents, the low wages and the peaceful labor conditions in this country but to invoice the articles produced here to selling organizations in Switzerland at the lowest possible prices and then to export these articles through those Swiss sales companies, which means that the major part of the profit will be made in Switzerland.'

"The Minister of Finance was asked whether fiscal concessions were granted which created unequal competition. He replied in the negative stating, in part, 'This is a phenomenon which is known to me, of course, and which I am actually watching with some concern also. A matter to be considered in this connection, however, is that, of course, we can better have a working company here than nothing at all, provided always that—and this is a matter which the Honorable

doing so have now been curtailed by recent changes in United States tax legislation.[28]

With regard to the balance-of-payments effects of these investments in European manufacturing, various and opposing influences may be distinguished. For one thing, they can be expected gradually to give rise to a return flow of earnings which—in time—will come to exceed the current rate of outflow of new capital from the United States into such enterprises. It is in this way that we now receive a large flow of income from our varied investments abroad built up over the past.[29] The remittance of earnings from current investment activity may be realized only after some years, however, and in the meantime the expansion of foreign manufacturing operations tends to produce both favorable and unfavorable effects on the balance of payments in other respects.

Concurrently with the act of foreign investment, we can discern certain positive consequences for United States exports, including demands for equipment and services as foreign manufacturing facilities are being constructed and demands for parts and materials as the plants begin to operate. In many cases, moreover, foreign manufacturing subsidiaries provide outlets for finished goods from this country to supplement their own more limited range of production. Along with these positive results certain negative effects may also be expected insofar as the expansion of American manufacturing operations abroad, including the development of ancillary supply functions, displaces products that would otherwise be exported from the United States.[30] Account must, however, be taken of the possibility that, in the absence of American investment, some of the productive capacity in question would be installed by others, with trade and employment effects on

---

Deputy, Mr. Hellema has mentioned, I believe—there will not be created an incorrect competitive basis for the new working company or against the existing Dutch industries . . .' " (John McCullough, *The Financial Executive*, *The Common Market and Taxes* [Lybrand, Ross Bros., and Montgomery], New York, 1960, p. 40).

[28] See pp. 74-75.

[29] Income from foreign investments has been one of the most rapidly growing elements among receipts over the past decade. See Table 6.

[30] The displacement of United States exports would tend to be increased (and the working of the price mechanism in international trade would be impeded) in cases where the United States company enters into arrangements with its foreign subsidiaries, or licensees, reserving to the latter the export market or a specified part of it. Such arrangements do not appear to be widespread, though little information is available on the subject.

the United States similar to those described, but with no return flow of earnings to this country.

It is possible that, in the recent growth of United States manufacturing investments in Western Europe, the expansionary effects on our trade have so far predominated. They may do so in the future, if our foreign subsidiaries prove to be effective export representatives as well as manufacturers. The net effect on our trade and on the balance of payments as a whole will depend in large measure on the over-all patterns which emerge with respect to the disposition of earnings from these new investments—that is, the extent to which they are remitted to the United States compared with the extent to which they are reinvested in the expansion of production facilities abroad. The inducements to invest in Western Europe are, however, very powerful for the various reasons which have been mentioned. We should not, therefore, underestimate the risk that the expansion of American manufacturing operations in this area may be proceeding in greater breadth and speed than would be consistent with our present trade and payments position. This question gains in importance because of the intimate connection which has been noted between these investments and the potential weakening of our role as a major supplier of technologically advanced products.

OFFICIAL MEASURES DIRECTLY AFFECTING BASIC TRANSACTIONS

The various official measures bearing directly on basic transactions have probably had little effect so far, at least prior to 1962, but may be felt increasingly from now on. Such measures tend to be either difficult to organize and execute or, once started, slow to produce results, or both.

It might seem that, in principle, government action could be brought to bear more quickly and effectively in reducing foreign expenditures, either its own or those of the private sector, than in increasing foreign receipts. In practice, the results obtained on the side of expenditures appear to have been modest so far. Apparently the growing urgency of the problems of Latin American and other less developed areas and threats to security in Berlin, Southeast Asia, and elsewhere have countered efforts to save on economic assistance and military expenditures abroad.

Government grants and loans for economic assistance were, in fact, at a rate more than $1 billion higher in 1961 and the first nine months of

1962 than two or three years earlier. The balance-of-payments impact of these outlays may have been softened by steps taken to tie procurement more closely to United States goods and services, though the time required for this action to be reflected in actual disbursements is rather long,[31] and the real effect is, for reasons already noted, difficult to evaluate.[32]

On a gross basis, military expenditures abroad have scarcely declined, except by comparison with the unusually high level of $3.4 billion in 1958. They have continued since then at an annual rate of about $3 billion. Even after a rigorous attempt to reduce foreign exchange outlays, including those of military and civilian personnel and their dependents, the Department of Defense estimates that gross military expenditures abroad will still total $2,865 million in fiscal year 1963, a reduction of only $178 million from fiscal year 1961. Savings on the side of expenditures are therefore expected to make only a modest contribution to the projected reduction of $1 billion in *net* military spending abroad in 1963.[33]

Probably the only action affecting government expenditures abroad that might have given prompt and substantial relief to the United States balance of payments would have been the assumption by Western European countries of a larger share in the costs of the common

[31] In mid-1962 disbursements were still being made on commitments undertaken before aid by the Development Loan Fund was tied in the fall of 1959.

[32] See p. 51.

[33] Announced as "a prime objective" by the Secretary of Defense on July 16, 1962. The Secretary further indicated that the reductions projected were expected to bring the net figure down to $1.6 billion by fiscal year 1963 and to $1 billion by fiscal year 1966. In testimony before the Joint Economic Committee on August 17, the Secretary of the Treasury indicated that the achievement of these targets would require "the full cooperation of our allies." More detailed figures on the targets were given on December 12, 1962, by Assistant Secretary of Defense Charles J. Hitch in testimony before the Subcommittee on International Exchange and Payments of the Joint Economic Committee. These figures show that the major contribution to the 1963 target is expected through an increase from $375 million to $1,244 million in U.S. military receipts (including "shipment of military supplies procured through the Department of Defense, reimbursement to the U.S. for logistical support of United Nations and other nations' defense forces and other sales of goods and services by the military departments"). Of the projected saving of $178 million in U.S. gross military outlays abroad, one-half would be in the operations of the "AEC and other agencies included in NATO definition of defense expenditures"; the other half would come chiefly from reductions in Department of Defense expenditures on its own construction programs abroad and on procurement and construction activities under the Military Assistance Program, offset in part by increases in various other items.

defense. A view on the adequacy of United States efforts in this regard goes well outside the scope of economic analysis and involves a nice judgment as to the real bargaining power of the leader of a rather loose and dissident alliance. The alternative of reducing American military forces in Europe would also imply a considered judgment on the ultimate political and military consequences of such a decision.

The possibilities for saving on civilian expenditures abroad by increasing customs duties or imposing quotas on imports are limited by the various commitments which we have undertaken in the interest of opening markets to our exports.[34] The risk of retaliation by other countries must also be kept in mind. A recent example was given when the Common Market countries doubled duties, effective August 1, 1962, on imports of a number of important items from the United States, but not on imports from other GATT members, in retaliation for the President's escape-clause action doubling U.S. duties on imports of sheet glass and wool carpeting.[35]

One of the few other possibilities for reducing private outlays abroad has involved proposals to change the rules governing taxation of foreign income. In April 1961 the administration proposed the elimination of deferral of tax with respect to the retained earnings of foreign subsidiaries operating in developed countries. It emphasized in this regard the need to reduce incentives to foreign investment afforded by operations in "tax havens" such as Switzerland. In October 1962, some nineteen months after the original proposal was made,

[34] Article II of the General Agreement on Tariffs and Trade provides that imports of items which have been the subject of negotiated concessions (i.e., reductions or bindings of import duties) under the Agreement shall be exempt from ordinary customs duties in excess of the negotiated rates. Articles XI and XII have the effect of prohibiting the use of quotas or other quantitative restrictions on imports except to safeguard the balance of payments—a provision which could scarcely be invoked by the United States without risk of putting pressure on the dollar in other ways. The same inhibition would arise with regard to the imposition of exchange restrictions on current transactions, for which the prior approval of the International Monetary Fund would be required under Article VIII of the Articles of Agreement.

[35] Duty rates were raised from 20 to 40 per cent on imports from the United States of polyethylene, polystyrene, and cloth of artificial fibers, from 21 to 40 per cent on cloth of synthetic fibers, and from 15 to 19 per cent on paints and varnishes. The United States, under Article XIX of GATT, had offered reductions on other commodities in compensation for the increase in duties on carpets and glass, but the Common Market countries, also invoking Article XIX, declared the offered compensation inadequate. See Department of Commerce, *International Commerce*, Washington, June 18, 1962, p. 48.

Congress passed legislation which curtailed tax haven operations, but without affecting the basic deferral of taxation for operating companies in developed countries.

Efforts to increase receipts seem to have given the most tangible results so far, especially in the government sector. These have included advance repayments of debt to the United States Government, though this is an exhaustible resource,[36] and the agreement with Western Germany and those expected to be signed with other countries for the purchase of military equipment and services from the United States.[37]

[36] From 1959 through the third quarter of 1962 prepayments of debt to the U.S. Government totaled close to $1.7 billion, more than 80 per cent of which was by countries of the Common Market. These countries, which for the time being would seem to be the most likely source of further prepayment, now owe the United States about $1.3 billion (exclusive of $200 million which Germany wants to offset against war claims on the United States), France accounting for some three-fourths of this figure. The United Kingdom owes the U.S. Government more than $4 billion, but would be a much less likely source of prepayments.

In retrospect, we may have learned too well the lesson of the debts from the First World War. Seen from the present vantage point in time, it might have proved useful if, on the aid extended after the Second World War, we had retained title to some of the counterpart funds in European currencies as contingent claims to be exercised, at our volition, in case of need. We could thereby have held large foreign exchange assets for currency stabilization operations and could also have provided from these funds the economic aid to the less developed countries which some European countries seem reluctant to extend, with indirect benefits to our own balance of payments. It may be noted in this connection that the total amount of grant aid extended by the United States after World War II (net of conversions to loans and of reverse grants and returns) came to $10.7 billion for countries now comprising the Common Market and $2.7 billion for the United Kingdom, not counting close to $11 billion of military supplies and services (Department of Commerce, *Foreign Grants and Credits by the United States' Government*, December 1961 Quarter, July 1962).

[37] In his statement on July 16, 1962, the Secretary of Defense referred to the agreement with the Federal Republic of Germany as one "by which the United States provides a cooperative logistics system for the armed forces of both countries and the Federal Republic of Germany will increase the level of military procurement in the United States and utilize American supply lines, depots, and mainte-nance and support facilities to fully offset the foreign exchange costs of maintaining our forces in Germany for a 2-year period." Assistant Secretary Hitch, in his testimony on December 12, stressed the importance of the undertaking by Germany (recently extended, he said, to cover the period through calendar year 1964) to offset our defense expenditures in that country, noting that these expenditures currently amount to $675-700 million a year. (This would not all be net gain, however, since Germany had previously been purchasing military items from the United States in smaller amounts.) Assistant Secretary Hitch further stated: "In addition, within the last few weeks, Italy has agreed to purchase over $100 million of military equipment from the United States as a first step toward offsetting our foreign exchange costs in that country. We are negotiating similar arrangements

The export drive, aimed at increasing the foreign exchange earnings of the private sector, has the great virtue of being addressed to the largest item in the balance of payments, so that even marginal results could be significant. In view of the time required for such an effort to arouse widespread interest and support, and the further time required for new business to be registered in actual deliveries, the program can scarcely have made much impact on the export figures so far, but, with the support of the newly expanded export credit insurance arrangements, it may become cumulatively effective.

Perhaps the most important change to the advantage of our exports since the adverse shift in the balance of payments has been the removal of the remaining quantitative import restrictions, in particular the discriminatory restrictions on goods from the dollar area, which other countries had imposed during the period of their own balance-of-payments difficulties. Most of these restrictions have now disappeared in Europe, with the notable exception of those on agricultural products, providing some visible benefits to our exports already and the opportunity to cultivate markets for goods which had previously been closely circumscribed. Japan has also made progress in liberalizing imports, but still maintains restrictions on a wide range of goods of significant trade interest.

At the same time, however, a new cause for concern arises because of the commercial policies of the members of the European Common Market. At an earlier stage, our attention was focused on the importance of creating a large European trading area with no internal barriers. Now, as the Common Market becomes more of a reality and attracts new adherents, we are increasingly concerned lest our ability to compete in it with our capital goods, our consumer manufactures, our industrial materials, and our foods be inhibited by its external tariffs and quotas. Even if we succeed in improving our

---

with other countries and contemplate approaching still others in the near future." He characterized the procurement of U.S. military equipment by our Allies as "the most promising method by which we can reduce the net adverse balance."

The balance-of-payments article in the December 1962 *Survey of Current Business* reports military receipts on two bases, Table 1 showing "military sales" of $96 million in the first quarter, $153 million in the second, and $168 million in the third, and Table 2 showing "military cash receipts" of $221 million in the first quarter, $241 million in the second, and $226 million in the third. The smaller figures are on a delivery basis, and the larger ones include, in addition, funds transferred to restricted accounts for military purchases to be made by foreign governments in the United States.

relative position by using the increased scope for negotiations provided by the Trade Expansion Act of 1962, we can scarcely hope to avoid some new strains and adjustments as the Common Market comes into being. The outlook for some of our important agricultural exports is especially disturbing.

There is also ground for concern that the commercial policies of many European countries may accord insufficient recognition to the need for the advanced nations to increase their imports from the less developed, low-wage countries,[38] and that the adjustments in trade and production necessary to this end may continue to fall unequally on the United States. Table 13 testifies to the disparities now prevailing in this regard. It will be noted that the table covers a number of labor-intensive products in which the low wages of the newly industrializing countries might be expected to give them a competitive advantage as contrasted with industries requiring greater inputs of capital and skill.[39] Imports of these products in 1959-1960 from all sources by the United States and by the Common Market (EEC) and the EFTA countries (including trade within these groups) were of roughly similar orders of magnitude. The United States, despite various restrictive measures, took 58 per cent of its total from Japan and other Asian countries, whereas the EFTA group took only 22 per cent and the Common Market group a mere 6 per cent from these sources. The absolute amounts, which may provide the most relevant comparisons, show that imports of these manufactures from Asian sources by the United States averaged close to $540 million per year, or almost two and a half times those of the EFTA countries and almost eight times those of the Common Market countries. Within the EFTA group, imports by the United Kingdom, with its special ties with some of the Asian

---

[38] These problems are examined in detail in Chapter V ("Europe and the Trade Needs of the Less Developed Countries") of United Nations Economic Commission for Europe, *Economic Survey of Europe in 1960*, Geneva, 1961.

[39] Japan, though now an industrialized nation, is included as a supplier in the table along with other Asian countries because its wages are still low compared with those in the United States and Western Europe, because the composition of its exports still shows many of the traits of a newly industrializing country, and because the United States and Western Europe would seem to share a political interest in developing trade with Japan rather than risk that it may become dependent on trade with Mainland China and other Communist countries or frustrated through inability, for lack of export outlets, to increase its imports sufficiently to support its economic growth.

TABLE 13

IMPORTS OF SELECTED MANUFACTURES BY THE UNITED STATES AND BY MEMBERS OF THE EUROPEAN ECONOMIC COMMUNITY AND OF THE EUROPEAN FREE TRADE AREA, TOTAL AND FROM THE FAR EAST, 1959-1960, ANNUAL AVERAGE

(millions of dollars)

SITC[a] Number	Commodity	United States		European Economic Community[b]		European Free Trade Area[c]	
		Total	From Far East[d]	Total	From Far East[d]	Total	From Far East[d]
651.03	Cotton yarn and thread, gray	2.1	—	27.8	—	32.6	7.2
652.01	Cotton fabrics, gray	33.9	21.5	43.4	12.5	111.8	77.8
653.04	Jute fabrics	100.9	90.1	5.3	2.0	24.9	18.8
656	Textile manufactures n.o.s.[e]	23.0	10.8	53.0	9.0	45.0	16.7
665	Glassware	22.5	3.4	49.7	.2	35.8	.8
666	Pottery	60.6	38.0	28.4	3.2	20.7	2.2
841	Clothing, excluding fur	272.9	183.2	229.2	20.2	248.1	52.2
851	Footwear	117.7	70.7	63.7	2.7	75.4	11.2
861	Scientific, optical, controlling instruments	72.0	26.9	149.0	7.4	153.4	9.0
899	Manufactured articles n.o.s.[e]	218.7	94.1	481.3	12.4	248.8	24.7
	Total of items listed	924.3	538.7	1,130.7	69.6	996.4	220.4

Elements of Strength and Weakness

countries, averaged $171 million, the only figure remotely comparable with that for the United States. Western Germany's imports averaged $35 million, accounting for one-half of the total for the Common Market, and France was at the foot of the list with an infinitesimal $1 million of imports of manufactures from Asian sources.

These differences might be explained in part by a smaller labor-cost advantage in Asian countries compared with Western Europe than compared with the United States, and perhaps also in part by a concentration of Asian sales efforts in the United States market. But it is also true (and of course relevant to the second of these points) that Western European countries have typically applied severe restrictions against imports of manufactures from Japan and other Asian sources. These restrictive policies, which so far show little evidence of significant relaxation, provide some basis for fears which have been expressed that the new regional grouping in Western Europe may show little concern for the needs and interests of the less privileged parts of the world. Given the chronic labor shortages which threaten to impede growth and foster inflation in most Western European countries, it would seem to be sensible if they were to decide, in their own interest, to import more freely of labor-intensive goods and thereby release manpower to industries of greater productivity.

4. *The Comparative Performance of Exports and Imports*

It is scarcely possible, at least without much further study, to disentangle the various influences which have been discussed and to measure their separate effects on our international competitive position. We may, however, consider the changes which have actually occurred over the last decade in our total exports and imports of goods and nonmilitary services as reflecting the combined impact of these and perhaps still other influences. It should also be useful to take a closer look at our performance in international trade in manufactured goods, since this is the area of major concern with respect to changes in our competitive position.

AN OVER-ALL VIEW: EXPORTS AND IMPORTS OF GOODS AND NONMILITARY SERVICES

In examining the relative changes in United States exports and imports of goods and nonmilitary services, the first problem is that of choosing an appropriate base period. In the discussion of this question at the end of Chapter II it was noted that there would be some advantage in extending the base to include a fairly long period, such as the six years 1950-1955. It seemed preferable, however, to omit the years most affected by the Korean war and to limit the base accordingly to 1953-1955. A choice is facilitated by the fact that, as indicated by Chart 9, it makes little difference whether one or the other base is taken.

On the surface, at least, the results summarized in Tables 14 and 15 indicate the need for some qualification of the view that the United States has suffered a serious deterioration in its international competitive position in recent years. A certain strengthening of that position would even appear to be suggested by the appreciably faster increase in exports than in imports both on merchandise account alone and on goods plus nonmilitary services. The surplus on these items has consequently increased by more than $3 billion—enough to offset the rise in the various other expenditures listed in Table 7, though still leaving the balance on basic transactions in deficit.

As far as these comparisons go, it would appear either that the forces tending to weaken the competitive position of the United States have been overstated or that they have been outweighed by other forces tending to strengthen it. Caution is, however, required with respect to the nature and permanence of some of these counterforces.

CHART 9

Payments and Receipts on Goods and Nonmilitary Services, 1925-1929 and 1935-1938, Annual Averages, and 1946 to 1962, Annually

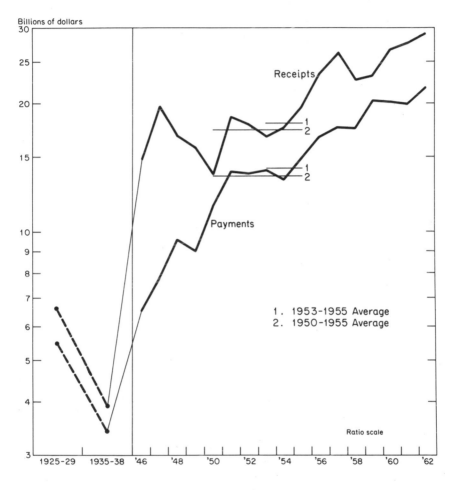

NOTE: 1962 data are for January-September, seasonally adjusted annual rate.

SOURCE: U.S. Department of Commerce.

For one thing, as has been noted, part of the increase in United States exports is accounted for by goods supplied directly under government aid programs. Data are not available for all such goods in earlier years, but certainly the greater part, especially within the time period considered, is represented by exports of agricultural products under our surplus disposal programs. An adjustment for these shipments, as given in the memorandum items at the bottom of Tables 14 and 15, reduces the percentage increase in exports since 1953-1955 (not, however, in relation to 1950-1955) but still leaves a decided advantage for exports compared with imports.

A further qualification is, however, needed to allow for that part of our exports in 1960 and 1961 made possible by the credits which were extended by American banks and business concerns and which figured prominently in the large outflows of short-term funds in those years.[40] An allowance for this influence, though difficult to estimate closely, would probably still leave the increase in exports to 1960-1961 greater than that in imports.[41] Credits by the United States serve to finance other countries' imports not only from this country but also from other sources, either directly in some cases or indirectly by releasing other funds available to the importing countries. Moreover, foreign borrowers are not without access to alternative sources of credit, including in particular the active Euro-dollar market operated by commercial banks in foreign financial centers and fed by the large official and unofficial dollar holdings accumulated abroad. Preliminary data for the first nine months of 1962, on the other hand, indicate that short-term credits played a much smaller role in financing exports during that period and, that accordingly, less qualification would be needed for this factor in the 1962 figures given in Tables 14 and 15.[42]

---

[40] See Table 5 and also the discussion on p. 37.

[41] For purposes of illustration, let it be assumed that 50 per cent of the reported short-term outflow in 1960 and 1961 as given in Table 5 (i.e., some $700 million in each year) made possible exports from the United States that otherwise would not have been made. A deduction of these exports, in addition to the adjustment already made for agricultural exports under special government programs, would reduce the increase in merchandise exports from 1953-1955 to 1960-1961 to 42 per cent (compared with 33.4 per cent for merchandise imports) and that for exports, including nonmilitary services, to 45.5 per cent (compared with 42.8 per cent for corresponding imports).

[42] Information is not yet available to permit an adjustment for agricultural exports under special government programs in 1962.

TABLE 14

PAYMENTS AND RECEIPTS ON GOODS AND NONMILITARY SERVICES
AND BALANCE ON BASIC TRANSACTIONS, BY SELECTED PERIODS, 1950 TO 1962

(millions of dollars, annual averages or annual rates)

	1950-1955	1953-1955	1960-1961	1962 Jan.-Sept.[a]
Payments				
Merchandise imports	10,670	10,957	14,618	16,109
Travel expenditures abroad	907	1,030	1,746 ⎱	⎱ 5,748
Other nonmilitary services	1,939	2,056	3,694 ⎰	⎰
Total, goods and nonmilitary services	13,516	14,043	20,058	21,857
Receipts				
Merchandise exports	12,820	13,120	19,687	20,772
Income on investments	1,981	2,194	3,452	4,035
Other nonmilitary services	2,516	2,665	4,030	4,363
Total, goods and nonmilitary services	17,317	17,979	27,169	29,170
Net receipts on goods and nonmilitary services	3,801	3,936	7,111	7,313
Net payments (—) on government transactions, private long-term investment, and remittances and pensions (from Table 7)[b]	—5,613	—5,644	—8,669	—8,615
Balance on basic transactions[b]	—1,812	—1,708	—1,558	—1,302
Memorandum items				
Agricultural exports under special government programs[c]	1,013	822	1,519	n.a.
Receipts adjusted to exclude agricultural exports under special government programs				
Merchandise exports	11,807	12,298	18,168	n.a.
Total, goods and nonmilitary services	16,304	17,157	25,669	n.a.

NOTES TO TABLE 14

NOTE: The adjustment made in the memorandum items do not entail a similar adjustment of the balance on basic transactions, since the transfer of these agricultural products is entered on both sides of the accounts (i.e., as a receipt for exports and as a payment under government grants and credits).

NOTES TO TABLE 14 (continued)

ᵃ Seasonally adjusted; preliminary data.

ᵇ Excludes unscheduled debt repayments to the U.S. Government (see Tables 1 and A-4).

ᶜ The exports excluded are those supplied under various government aid programs (such as the European Recovery Program, Mutual Security Program, etc.); U.S. Department of Agriculture donations and barter deals, starting in 1950; and Public Law 480 for the disposal of surplus farm products, starting in 1954. The figures do not include "shipments of some commodities with governmental assistance in the form of (1) extension of credit for relatively short periods, sales of government-owned commodities at less than domestic market prices, and (3) export payments in cash or in kind." (See U.S. Department of Agriculture, Economic Research Service Report No. 84, June 1961, and other reports in the same series.)

The amount excluded for 1950-1955 is the average for the seven-year period July 1949 – June 1956, and the amount excluded for 1953-1955 is the average for the four-year period July 1952 – June 1956, data not being available for these years on a calendar-year basis.

SOURCE: U.S. Department of Commerce.

COMPETITIVE POSITION IN TRADE IN MANUFACTURES

The relatively favorable performance of our exports compared with that of our imports of goods and nonmilitary services is not necessarily inconsistent with a much more pessimistic hypothesis about our position in international competition, especially with regard to trade in manufactured products. To bring together various doubts that have been expressed in this regard, this hypothesis might be formulated as follows: that costs and prices in the United States are out of line with those of its leading competitors; that market imperfections, however, retard shifts in trade in response to these disparities; that, for the time being, the more rapid increase in incomes in other industrial countries than in the United States has tended to keep our exports rising in relation to our imports; that, for these reasons, the United States may have benefited so far from its higher prices through gains in the terms of trade more than it has lost through the impairment of its competitive position;[43] that, however, the erosive effects of our unfavorable price

[43] In other words, the suggestion is that, under the conditions specified, foreign demand for United States exports has been relatively inelastic in the short run, and that total export proceeds have been greater than they would have been had export prices not risen in relation to import prices. However, if foreign demand has, in fact, been relatively elastic, a lower level of export prices would have served to increase the quantity of exports enough to yield a greater total return than that actually realized.

TABLE 15

PERCENTAGE INCREASE IN PAYMENTS AND RECEIPTS ON GOODS AND
NONMILITARY SERVICES

	Measured from 1950-1955		Measured from 1953-1955	
	1960-1961	1962 Jan.-Sept.	1960-1961	1962 Jan.-Sept.
Payments				
Merchandise imports	37.0	51.0	33.4	47.0
Travel expenditures abroad	92.5 ⎱	102.0	69.5 ⎱	86.3
Other nonmilitary services	90.5 ⎰		70.7 ⎰	
Total, goods and nonmilitary services	48.4	61.7	42.8	55.6
Receipts				
Merchandise exports	53.6	62.0	50.1	58.3
Income on investments	74.3	103.7	57.3	83.9
Other nonmilitary services	60.2	73.4	51.2	63.7
Total, goods and nonmilitary services	56.9	68.4	51.1	62.2
Memorandum items (receipts adusted to exclude agricultural exports under special government programs)				
Merchandise exports	53.9	n.a.	47.7	n.a.
Total, goods and nonmilitary services	57.4	n.a.	49.6	n.a.

SOURCE: Table 14.

position will be increasingly felt and may be accentuated to the extent
that the United States succeeds in raising its level of employment and
its rate of growth in relation to those of other industrial countries.

That part of this formulation concerning market imperfections was
developed with great cogency by Yntema in a statement published at
the beginning of 1960:

. . . . On the basis of fragmentary evidence, it seems to me that our exchange
rates are incompatible with the fundamental relation between costs of production
here and abroad. The effects on our balance of payments resulting from the disparities in costs here and abroad are limited now by market imperfections—by

lack of knowledge, inadequate procurement arrangements abroad by U.S. purchasers and inadequate distribution systems here for foreign producers. In the future the effects of these disparities in costs will be felt increasingly as foreign capacities expand, as economies of scale in production and distribution of foreign products increase, as more U.S. know-how is exported, as U.S. procurement abroad becomes more efficient (and more extensive) and as distribution systems for foreign products in the U.S. improve.[44]

Yntema's statement was drafted in the shadow of the extremely adverse trade and payments developments of 1958 and 1959 depicted in Chapter II and loses something in force by virtue of the subsequent recovery of 28 per cent in merchandise exports as against a rise of 5 per cent in imports (from 1959 to the first nine months of 1962, annual rate). The view expressed may nevertheless correctly characterize certain important elements in our foreign trade position. The growth of our imports of manufactures suggests that the frictions to which Yntema alluded are being overcome, and that further penetration of the American market by some of these and perhaps still other products can be expected.[45] Though his statement seems to refer only to imports, similar forces are no doubt working to displace some of our exports. The question, however, is how extensive and pervasive are these forces? Are they dominant, or are they offset by other forces? And are the disturbances persistent and continuing, or do they tend to stimulate corrective reactions?

It is a mark of the inadequacy of our factual knowledge and analytical capacities that answers to questions such as these remain so largely subject to conjecture and contention. In this connection, note may be taken of one set of data widely cited as evidence of a strongly unfavorable trend in the competitive power of the United States—that is, the progressive decline in its share of total world exports of

---

[44] From a footnote of dissent by Theodore O. Yntema in a Committee for Economic Development brochure, *National Objectives and the Balance of Payments Problem*, New York, 1960, pp. 3-4.

[45] It is understood that some American companies have found it cheaper, for like qualities, to procure various items of materials and equipment abroad for their foreign operations, but nevertheless continue to patronize their traditional domestic suppliers for their requirements in this country. Such private "Buy American" policies could, however, give way in time, if price differentials persist. On the other hand, it would seem plausible to suppose that similar market imperfections abroad (including those created by the formerly severe restrictions against imports of nonessentials from this country) may handicap our own exports and could be made to yield to an energetic export drive.

manufactures from 27 per cent in 1950 to about 25 per cent in the mid-50's and 20 or 21 per cent at present. By this standard, the United States has indeed lost in competitive position. But one must be clear about what the standard measures. It reflects, as a major component of the decline, the fact that some countries, especially Western Germany and Japan, still had an abnormally low share in world production and trade at the beginning of the 1950's. The subsequent rapid increase in their production and imports had to be accompanied by a rapid increase also in their exports—in fact, an even more rapid increase in exports than in imports unless they were to continue to receive financial assistance from the United States or elsewhere. No figures on market shares drawn from the past, whether the early postwar years or some prior period, are necessarily appropriate to our circumstances of today, but the data presented in Chart 10 put the matter in longer historical perspective. In relation to any of the years shown prior to World War II, it is not the United States but rather the United Kingdom that has lost ground in world trade in manufactures and made way, so to speak, for the gains of others, not only Western Germany and Japan but also the smaller industrial countries.[46]

It is true, however, that the decline in the United States share in world exports of manufactures in the last few years includes another component reflecting the important fact that its exports have not risen enough, or its imports too much, to meet the increase in its international financial load and at the same time close the gap in its international payments. To relate the figures on market shares to the problem at hand, one may say that—if the whole of the deficit on basic transactions in the first nine months of 1962 were to have been eliminated exclusively by changes in our trade in manufactures—the share of the United States in world exports of these goods (totaling some $57 billion, annual rate) would have needed to be higher by about 2 to 2.5 percentage points, achieved either by larger exports of its own or by smaller imports of other countries' exports of manufactures. It is this figure, suggesting sufficient problems in itself, rather than the 6 or 7 percentage-point decline since 1950 that gives some indication of the strengthening needed in our competitive position in

[46] On the basis of recent trends, however, the National Institute of Economic and Social Research (London) suggests that "the downward trend in Britain's share in world trade in manufactures may at last have been halted" (*Economic Review*, November 1962, pp. 10, 11).

CHART 10

World Exports of Manufactured Goods, Selected Years, 1913 to 1962

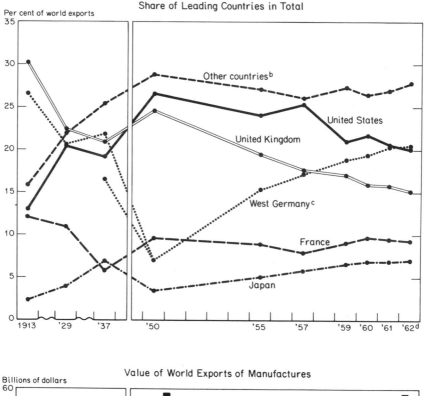

Share of Leading Countries in Total

Per cent of world exports

Other countries[b]

United States

United Kingdom

West Germany[c]

France

Japan

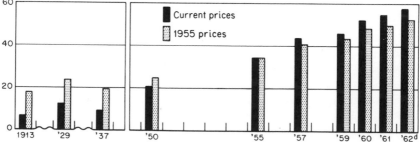

Value of World Exports of Manufactures

Billions of dollars

■ Current prices

▨ 1955 prices

Elements of Strength and Weakness

ᵃ Commodity composition corresponds to Sections 5 to 8 of the United Nations' Standard International Trade Classification. Exports from countries of the Soviet bloc are not included.

ᵇ Belgium-Luxembourg, Canada, India, Italy, Netherlands, Sweden, and Switzerland, except that the Netherlands is not included in 1913 and India is not included in 1960 and subsequently.

ᶜ The lower point shown for 1937 is based on the estimated share of the area now comprising the Federal Republic in total German exports of manufactures in 1937. The higher point for 1937 and also the points for 1913 and 1929 relate to the whole of Germany as of each of those years.

ᵈ Data for first six months, seasonally adjusted. The unadjusted figures are: U.S., 20.7; West Germany, 19.9; U.K., 15.6; France, 9.5; Japan, 6.8; other countries, 27.5.

SOURCE: (1) For years 1913-1959: Forthcoming study on *Industrialization and International Trade* by Alfred Maizels, London, National Institute of Economic and Social Research, except as noted in 3. (2) For years 1960-1962: *Economic Review,* London, National Institute of Economic and Social Research, November 1962, p. 59, except as noted in 3. (3) Value of world trade at 1955 prices in 1960, 1961, and 1962 computed from price index for world exports of manufactured goods given in *Monthly Bulletin of Statistics,* United Nations, June 1962, p. viii. Value of world trade at 1955 prices in 1913 is derived from a series in Maizels' study computed in 1913 prices.

manufactures for purposes of bolstering the balance of payments.

Something of the nature of the problem facing the United States in strengthening its competitive position in manufactures is indicated by the relative course of its exports and imports of these products over the past decade. The series given in the first part of Chart 11 show that the absolute rise in exports of manufactures, including semi-manufactures,[47] has been greater than that in imports. The rise in the excess of exports over imports is, however, small—a gain of about $1.3 billion in the annual averages for the period 1960 through the first three quarters of 1962 over the averages for 1953-1955. For finished manufactures only, the gain was little more than $400 million. It is also evident from the same series plotted on a ratio scale in the second part of the chart that, in percentage terms, the rate of increase in imports of manufactures, especially of finished manufactures, has been

[47] The groupings given in Chart 11 are from the arrangement by "economic classes" of the Department of Commerce. The series for finished manufactures is somewhat narrower, but that including semimanufactures somewhat broader, than the definition of manufactures in Chart 10, which is derived from the Standard International Trade Classification developed by the United Nations.

CHART 11

U.S. Trade in Finished Manufactures and Semimanufactures

A. Arithmetic Scale

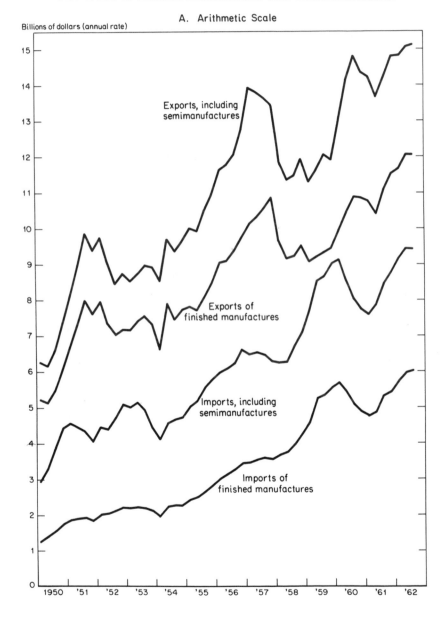

Billions of dollars (annual rate)

Exports, including
semimanufactures

Exports of
finished manufactures

Imports, including
semimanufactures

Imports of
finished manufactures

CHART 11 (concluded)

B. Ratio Scale

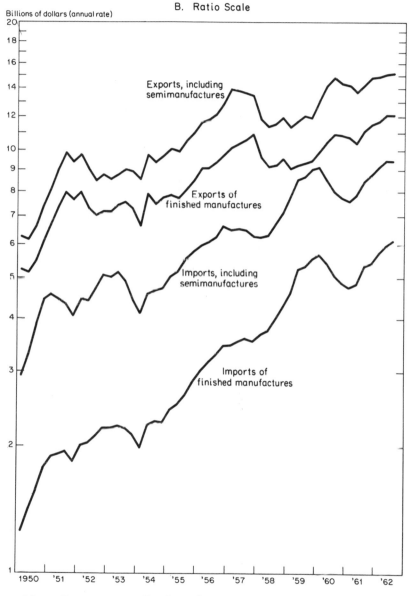

Billions of dollars (annual rate)

Exports, including semimanufactures

Exports of finished manufactures

Imports, including semimanufactures

Imports of finished manufactures

NOTE: Data are seasonally adjusted.

SOURCE: U.S. Department of Commerce.

91

TABLE 16

UNITED STATES FOREIGN TRADE IN RESEARCH-INTENSIVE PRODUCTS[a]
(millions of dollars, annual averages or annual rates)

	1926-1935	1953-1955	1956-1957	1958-1959	1960-1961	1962 Jan.-Sept.[b]	Percentage Increase from 1953-1955 to 1960-1961	Percentage Increase from 1953-1955 to 1962 Jan.-Sept.[b]
I-A. U.S. exports, including special category Type II[c]								
Total exports, all products	3,338	14,307	19,300	17,067	20,163	21,046	41	47
Exports of research-intensive products (percentage of total)	780 (23.4)	6,508 (45.5)	8,438 (43.7)	8,056 (47.2)	9,417 (46.7)	10,533 (50.0)	45	62
Construction, excavating, and mining machinery	40	492	845	695	768	838	56	70
Other industrial machinery	110	1,054	1,482	1,545	1,861	2,192	77	108
Electrical apparatus	83	869	1,023	1,003	1,072	1,245	23	43
Office machines and parts	33	93	122	139	260	331	180	256
Scientific and professional instruments	8	63	97	99	118	144	87	129
Photographic and projection goods	20	80	102	109	137	153	71	91
Agricultural implements	31	129	130	134	144	166	12	29
Tractors, parts and accessories	37	332	385	333	373	372	12	12
Automobiles, parts and accessories	277	1,347	1,499	1,281	1,240	1,292	−8	−4
Aircraft, parts and accessories	8	745	1,047	878	1,282	1,499	72	101
Railway transportation equipment	13	110	127	157	150	162	36	47
Synthetic fibers and manufactures	5	223	248	250	307	326	38	46
Medicinal and pharmaceutical preparations	16	229	265	281	275	269	20	17
Chemicals and related products[d]	99	742	1,066	1,152	1,430	1,544	93	108

(continued)

TABLE 16 (concluded)

	1926-1935	1953-1955	1956-1957	1958-1959	1960-1961	1962 Jan.-Sept.b	Percentage Increase from 1953-1955 to 1960-1961	Percentage Increase from 1953-1955 to 1962 Jan.-Sept.b
I-B. U.S. exports, excluding special category Type II								
Total exports, all products	3,338	12,623	17,847	15,753	18,782	19,180	49	52
Exports of research-intensive productse (percentage of total)	780 (23.4)	5,379 (42.6)	7,198 (40.3)	6,988 (44.4)	8,269 (44.0)	8,906 (46.4)	54	66
Electrical apparatus	83	635	786	807	842	894	33	41
Automobiles, parts and accessories	277	1,081	1,334	1,116	1,170	1,177	8	9
Aircraft and aircraft engines	8	131	225	188	451	361	244	176
Chemicals and related products	99	727	1,050	1,135	1,413	1,521	94	109
II. U.S. imports								
Total imports, all products	2,868	10,821	12,949	14,310	14,821	16,044	37	48
Imports of research-intensive products (percentage of total)	138 (4.8)	684 (6.3)	1,075 (8.3)	1,784 (12.5)	1,885 (12.7)	2,168 (13.5)	176	217
Industrial machinery	n.a.	107	145	152	228	283	113	164
Electrical apparatus	15	48	122	206	293	394	510	721
Office machines and parts	n.a.	10	30	42	83	80	730	700
Scientific and professional instruments	2	15	26	33	44	52	193	247
Photographic goods	4	23	37	46	58	71	152	209
Agricultural implements and parts	5	76	78	146	124	152	63	100
Automobiles and parts	2	64	241	699	503	489	686	664
Aircraft and parts	—	30	70	73	107	134	257	347
Synthetic fibers and manufactures	9	45	51	72	73	100	62	122
Chemicals and related products	101	266	275	315	372	413	40	55

NOTES TO TABLE 16

ᵃ The selection of "research-intensive" goods is that given for U.S. exports by Erik Hoffmeyer, *Dollar Shortage and the Structure of U.S. Foreign Trade,* Copenhagen and Amsterdam, 1958, pp. 189-190.

ᵇ Not seasonally adjusted.

ᶜ "Special category" goods of Type II are selected items for which, under national security restrictions, details are published by commodity but not by country. "Special category" goods of Type I are those for which only totals are published, without distribution by commodity or by country, and are not included above. A list of the items in these groups is given in report FT 410 for January 1961, issued by the Bureau of the Census.

ᵈ Excluding medicinal and pharmaceutical preparations.

ᵉ Product groups shown are limited to those affected by the exclusion of "special category" items. Others remain as in part I-A of the table.

SOURCE: Arranged from trade statistics published by the Department of Commerce.

much greater than that in exports. A continuation of these percentage increases would, of course, eventually make the absolute gain in imports exceed that in exports, but the rather uncertain course taken by both series in the last four or five years warns against any such simple projection.

Much the same observations can be made if we examine, in the light of Table 16, the development of United States trade in "research-intensive" goods, taking for this purpose the groups selected by Hoffmeyer.[48] Before World War II, imports of these goods made up only a small part of total imports and consisted chiefly of chemicals. In recent years, they have increased rapidly, trebling from 1953-1955 to 1962, and now include a wider range of goods. Exports of research-intensive products, though rising only 60 per cent during this time, still exceeded imports by $6.7 billion in 1962 (January-September,

[48] See discussion on p. 53. As noted there, one may question whether competitive strength in these goods is mainly attributable to the amount of research incorporated in them or to other factors, such as size and growth of markets, conditioning the development of large-scale industry. However that may be, it is still of interest to observe the growth of United States exports and imports of these technologically advanced products.

It may be noted that Hoffmeyer applied his research-intensive criterion only to exports—an indication of the relatively small role which these products played in United States imports through the period (ending in 1955) covered by his study. In Table 16, however, his selection of items is applied also to imports (though presented in slightly more summary form than exports in the table).

annual rate), or $2 billion more than in 1953-1955.[49]

Both imports and exports of research-intensive goods seem to show a certain retardation in the last few years. That in imports, it will be noted, is largely due to the fall in automobiles after the 1959 peak, an experience which suggests that the resistance of domestic producers tends to stiffen as the share of the market taken by imports increases. A number of other items in the import list may, however, have some distance to go before this point is reached.

The geographic distribution given in Chart 12[50] suggests that the slowing down in United States exports of research-intensive goods is largely attributable to the weakness in these exports to Canada and Latin America since 1956 and 1957, when investment in resource development reached a peak and created heavy demands for construction and mining machinery and other capital equipment. Exports to industrial countries, on the other hand, have continued to increase strongly and almost trebled from 1952 to 1960, though the upsurge in the latter year was influenced by the concentration of deliveries of jet aircraft. With a sustained, though much slower, rise in exports to still other countries, markets outside the Western Hemisphere now take more than half of total United States exports of research-intensive goods compared with about 40 per cent ten years ago.

Apart from such favorable or unfavorable implications as may be read from the statistical record, the analysis given in this chapter suggests various reasons for thinking that the increase in imports of manufactures may become less spectacular in relation to the rise in exports, and that the United States has a good possibility of continuing to

[49] These figures exclude exports in special category Type II. Inclusive of these exports, the excess of exports rose from $5.9 billion in 1953-1955 to $8.4 billion in 1962 (January-September, annual rate).

In a special study of U.S. exports, the *Survey of Current Business* for December 1962 finds a striking trend toward increased sales of highly specialized industrial equipment since 1959. Increased foreign demand for technologically advanced and custom-made types of equipment, the article states, is illustrated by the dramatic gains scored in recent years by such exports as paper and packaging machinery, plastic-making machinery, seamless-hosiery machinery, a variety of machine tools, electronic computers, measuring and testing instruments, and research laboratory apparatus. The article also notes, however, a growing tendency for domestic manufacturers to supply foreign demand from assembly plants and other manufacturing facilities abroad rather than from the United States.

[50] Exports of "special category—Type II" are plotted separately, since they are not available in country detail.

CHART 12

U.S. Exports of Research-Intensive Goods by Destination, 1952-1961

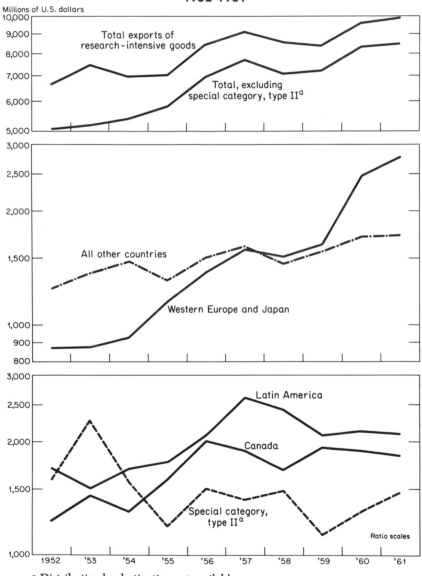

Millions of U.S. dollars

Total exports of research-intensive goods

Total, excluding special category, type II[a]

All other countries

Western Europe and Japan

Latin America

Canada

Special category, type II[a]

Ratio scales

a Distribution by destination not available.

NOTE: See Table 16 for items included in research-intensive goods.

SOURCE: U.S. Department of Commerce.

increase its export surplus in this major area of competition. These reasons include the fact that our exports of technologically advanced goods are still more broadly based than our imports, so that we may experience adverse shifts in our trade in various items and still gain on balance; the pressures on producers affected by increased imports or loss of exports to make a competitive response, including the search for ways of reducing costs and improving products; the tendency for wages and other costs to rise in Europe under conditions of high utilization of plant and manpower capacity; and the efforts made by the Government to promote exports which are probably only now beginning to bear fruit but may do so increasingly henceforth.

5. *Growth and the Balance of Payments*

As long as other leading industrial countries continue to operate at high levels of capacity utilization,[51] increases in their exports may be difficult to achieve without increases in their imports or further upward pressures on their costs.[52] These are, incidentally, reasons why

[51] If, under these conditions, their rate of growth slows down for lack of manpower, some types of imports would presumably grow more slowly or even decline, but not necessarily imports of labor-saving machinery and materials.

A prospective leveling out of United States exports of machinery may be indicated by the recent behavior of the McGraw-Hill index of export orders for nonelectrical machinery, the only comprehensive series of its nature with respect to the range of products covered. The index (1957=100) fell from 177 in July 1962 to 154 in August and September, below the level of a year earlier. A recovery to 175 in October, however, brought the average for the four months to 165 compared with 166 for the first six months of the year and 161 for the first and second halves of 1961. On the other hand, the index is still at a very high level compared with the average of 121 for the whole of 1960. For a discussion of the McGraw-Hill export order index and related series, see the 1962 Annual Report of the National Bureau of Economic Research, pp. 96-98.

[52] In this connection, it may be noted that the total merchandise imports of the Common Market countries increased 11 per cent compared with a rise of 6 per cent in their total merchandise exports in the first nine month of 1962 in relation to the same period of 1961. The absolute figures are as follows (annual rates, not seasonally adjusted):

	Imports, c.i.f.	Exports, c.i.f.
	(billions of dollars)	
1961 (January-September)	31.5	31.6
1962 (January-September)	35.0	33.4

SOURCE: International Monetary Fund, *International Financial Statistics*, October 1962, pp. 38, 39; December 1962, pp. 38, 39.

the effects of the Common Market on United States exports, at least of manufactures, may be less severe than could be supposed from the difference in tariff treatment accorded imports from outside compared with trade among the members: to the extent that their trade with each other grows still faster than it would in the absence of preferential treatment, they will need either to slacken the growth of their exports to outside countries or to accelerate their imports from them.

A reduction in the disparity between American and European employment levels and growth rates caused by a slack in Europe would undoubtedly affect United States trade adversely, possibly offset in some measure, as far as the balance of payments is concerned, by changes in the flow of investment funds. Impressions of the vulnerability of the United States to such a situation may, however, have been exaggerated by the 1958 experience, when various attendant circumstances greatly accentuated the fall in United States exports.[53]

A higher level of employment and faster rate of growth in the United States, activity in Europe continuing on more or less the present upward course, would also tend to affect the trade balance adversely, this time through increases in United States imports, possibly offset in its balance-of-payments effects by the enhanced attraction of investing in this country compared with Europe. Such a strengthening of the American economy should also, however, have some stimulating effect on third countries, notably our major trading partners in the Western Hemisphere. It should thus react favorably on our own exports, particularly since the supply position in the United States is so much easier than in other industrial countries and should allow room, at present, for increases in both domestic and foreign sales.

Perhaps the most important question relevant to the future development of our international position is whether we will be able to succeed in maintaining stability of the general price level under conditions of higher employment and more rapid growth. It may be that the relative improvement in our cost and price position vis-à-vis Europe over the past three or four years is no more than can be explained by the unsatisfactory levels of employment and corporate profits in the United States during this time.

[53] See pp. 30-32 above.

Chapter IV

The Search for Ways of Strengthening
Our International Payments Position

---

1. *Future Uncertainties and the Need for Flexibility*

The United States faces the twofold problem of eliminating the present deficit in its international accounts and of strengthening its position to meet future contingencies. It is not possible to distinguish sharply between these two aspects of the problem. The discussion in the preceding chapters shows how difficult it is to appraise the various forces currently influencing our international position. We cannot generalize with certainty about our cost and price levels in relation to those of other countries—factual information on this subject is weak and fragmentary, and pronouncements about it inevitably contain a large element of subjective judgment. Attempts to appraise our situation in this respect at any time in the last several years could not properly have overlooked the growing tightness of the labor market in European countries and its implications for their production costs, just as, today, we are not entitled to assume that we have now found the answer to cost and price stability in this country. Nor, to take another variable in the present scene, can we know for sure what effects are currently being produced by the recent wave of expansion of American manufacturing operations in Europe and how, on balance, they may be influencing this country's international trade and payments position.

The dynamics of the present merge with the uncertainties of the future. Assessments of our prospects must try to allow for the effects of forces which can now be only dimly perceived. Will the less developed countries, faced with a discouraging outlook for their traditional exports of primary products, turn increasingly to the development of those kinds of manufacturing industries in which their abundant low-cost labor may give them a comparative advantage in international trade? And will they find markets receptive to their manufactures? Will the countries of the Soviet bloc, with their stubborn emphasis on heavy industry both for military reasons and for more obscure ideological predilections, seek to increase their exports of capital goods to countries aspiring to economic development and take in return both food and manufactured consumer goods in which their own production remains deficient? Will the growing concentration of economic power in the European Common Market be used aggressively to protect production within the area and to enhance its bargaining position vis-à-vis outsiders? Or will that power be accompanied by a commensurate sense of responsibility for sharing military burdens and for assisting in the development of the countries which have lagged behind and need not only financial assistance but also greater freedom to export to the wealthier nations?

Will our technological advantages be reinforced by our large expenditures on research, including side benefits from defense-oriented outlays, or will the accelerated transmission of ideas and capital quickly diffuse these results to other countries with little benefit to our own foreign trade? Does the apparent resistance which many European countries have shown to recession in recent years manifest a superior skill in devising and using the tools of economic policy? Or will the filling out of their industrial structures make them more susceptible to business cycles and less reliable as markets for United States exports?[1]

Efforts to measure the present "hard core" deficit or to project the future evolution of the balance of payments may be a useful exercise in giving quantitative expression to those influences which can be more or less clearly identified. But one could scarcely assign a high degree of probability to such estimates, no matter how refined the methods employed, in view of the importance of those influences which cannot be assessed and in view of the nature of the balance of payments as "a marginal part of a marginal part." To quote Sir Donald MacDougall further: "...I have come to the conclusion that the only thing which can be said with certainty about any country's balance of

---

[1] For an interesting exchange on this point, see the paper presented by Milton Gilbert, and Walter Salant's comments on it, at the American Economic Association meeting in December 1961 (*Papers and Proceedings*, May 1962, pp. 93-110, 119-122).

payments is that it changes when one least expects it, and often in the opposite direction."[2]

The significance of these inevitable uncertainties is that we need to strengthen our capacity to adjust to changing circumstances, to search for ways of introducing more flexibility into the international payments system, and to recognize that, in spite of all that we may do, there will be periods of strain. These strains need not be all in one direction—with a favorable break we may yet see the setting for a revival of a somewhat chastened "chronic dollar shortage" school. But we have to reckon with the possibility that new disturbances may add to the strains we have already experienced.

2. *Limitations on Lines of Action Open to the United States*

An appraisal of our ability to face these uncertainties needs to start with a recognition of the limitations on the measures which the United States can invoke to strengthen its balance of payments. These limitations apply, though not uniquely, with peculiar force to this country because of the size and other characteristics of its economy, its role in world affairs, and the status of the dollar as the world's leading reserve currency. Later, the European Common Market may be subject to somewhat similar limitations, if it develops a unified economy and external policies appropriate to its position, but that is for the future to tell.

At present, the situation is that the United States needs to be mindful of the effects which its policies may have on other countries, but to show considerable restraint if their policies tend to aggravate its own difficulties. Not only the United States but various other countries as well, both large and small, are at one time or another in balance-of-payments difficulty. To strengthen the position of the United States at their expense would, in many cases, tend to increase its burdens in other ways. Thus, we avoid cutting local procurement by our military forces in South Korea, since to do so would only force us to find other means of helping to meet that country's need for foreign exchange. Other countries, even major ones, may feel less restraint. For instance, Canada, facing the problem during the early part of 1962 of arresting the fall of the Canadian dollar and defending the new parity set in

[2] *The Dollar Problem: A Reappraisal*, p. 64.

May, was able not only to obtain special credits from the United States but also to apply surcharges on about one-half of its total imports.

The limitations to which the United States is especially subject may be further considered with respect to the possibility of recourse to deflation or to a change in exchange rates—two of the principal methods traditionally employed for correcting balance-of-payments deficits.[3]

LIMITATIONS ON RECOURSE TO DEFLATION

Perhaps no country today would regard deflation as a preferred and usual way of adjusting its balance of payments. Yet, under sufficiently adverse circumstances, some countries might consider a business contraction as a necessary means, or a necessary adjunct to other policies, to reduce costs and prices or, at least, to combat further increases. Even if it were otherwise prepared to follow such a course, the United States, more than any other country, must consider the impact of its action on its trading partners. This is not simply a matter of concern for their welfare or for good political relations but also a question of eventual adverse repercussions on this country's own exports, on capital movements, and on foreign needs for financial assistance. Smaller countries would have much less, or no, reason to worry about such repercussions.

These problems may be illustrated by reference to the 1960-61 recession in the United States, which had been preceded by a sharp turn in federal fiscal policy and a tightening of credit inspired largely by concern for the balance of payments and the threat to the dollar.[4]

---

[3] With respect to yet another method frequently employed to combat balance-of-payments deficits—that is, quantitative controls or increased duties on imports —it has been noted in Chapter III (p. 74) that the United States is restricted in its freedom of action not only by the commitments entered into jointly with other countries under the IMF and GATT but also, and perhaps even more severely, by the risk of retaliation by other countries. As the country with the largest total trade and the largest merchandise export surplus (even if inadequate to cover private foreign investments and government operations abroad), the United States is probably more exposed than smaller countries to retaliatory action, should it attempt to apply a generally restrictive policy to imports except, perhaps, under conditions of manifest emergency.

[4] For a discussion of the role of restrictive fiscal and credit policies in halting the 1958-1960 expansion, see Arthur F. Burns, "Examining the New 'Stagnation' Theory," *The Morgan Guaranty Survey*, May 1961, pp. 4-5.

The recession doubtless served to arrest an "inflationary psychology," which might have difficult to accomplish in any other way. It may thereby have helped—in conjunction with the inflationary pressures in Western Europe and Japan generated by their business boom—to lay the basis for an improvement in our competitive position. But any immediate benefits to our international payments position through the reduction of imports[5] may have been offset by the effects on the buying power and general economic condition of some of our principal trading partners in the Western Hemisphere[6] and by the stimulus given to American investment in Western Europe. A more obvious development bearing unfavorably on the balance of payments was the great outflow of liquid funds as the Federal Reserve relaxed credit conditions with the onset of the recession—a consequence which, however, might be avoided under a different combination of policies, as discussed in Section 4 of this chapter.

There is a particular reason why the United States may find it more difficult than other countries to employ deflation as a means of balance-of-payments adjustment. Though it is the world's largest exporter and importer, the United States is *sui generis* among the developed countries of the non-Communist world with respect to the size of foreign trade in its own economy. As may be seen in Table 17, the ratio of exports or imports of goods and services to gross national product ranges elsewhere from as low as about 12 per cent in Japan to around 15 per cent in France and Italy, to 20 or 25 per cent in Germany and the United Kingdom, and on up to about 35 per cent in Belgium and as much as 50 per cent in the Netherlands. In the United States the ratio is a mere 5 per cent.

The usual assumption seems to be that a country in which foreign trade plays so modest a role should have less difficulty than most in making necessary adjustments in its external accounts. Triffin, for instance, says: "The relatively small role of external transactions in relation to GNP, and the enormous strength and resiliency of our

---

[5] Nor could all of the decline in United States imports coinciding with the recession be attributed to it. The large drop in automobile imports, for one thing, probably owed much more to Detroit's introduction of the compact car and to a switch from accumulation to decumulation of dealers' inventories of imported models.

[6] See Chapter II, p. 34.

TABLE 17

EXPORTS AND IMPORTS OF GOODS AND SERVICES IN RELATION
TO GROSS NATIONAL PRODUCT, UNITED STATES AND
SELECTED FOREIGN COUNTRIES, AVERAGE FOR 1959-1961

| | Percentage of Gross National Product | |
Country	Exports	Imports
United States	5.1	4.5
Japan	12.0	10.3
France	15.8	14.7
Italy	16.8	15.7
Australia[a]	17.1	17.8
Canada	19.7	22.8
United Kingdom	23.5	23.2
Germany, Fed. Rep.	24.6	21.8
Sweden	26.5	26.8
Belgium[b]	35.0	32.9
Netherlands[b]	51.9	48.3

[a] Years ending June 30.
[b] 1958-1960 average.

SOURCE: Australia, International Monetary Fund, *International Financial Statistics*, November 1962; Japan, Bureau of Statistics, Office of the Prime Minister, *Monthly Statistics of Japan*, July 1962; all other countries, OECD, *General Statistics*, September 1962 and 1961.

economy, should facilitate these necessary adjustments, and rule out difficulties of the kind previously encountered by Britain."[7]

Southard has suggested a contrary view,[8] one which seems particularly relevant to the adjustments needed to accommodate large increases in economic assistance, foreign military expenditures, and

[7] *Gold and the Dollar Crisis*, p. 68.

[8] ". . . the relatively small percentage relationship between balance-of-payments magnitudes and GNP in the United States probably gives rise to sluggishness in the responsiveness of the American economy to the impact of even large deficits or surpluses in the balance of payments. Income changes are the principal element in the mechanism of adjustment, and it must be presumed that those changes will have relatively small effect on the United States, where, for example, total imports or exports are only about 5 per cent of GNP" (Frank A. Southard, Jr., "United States Experience," in "The Discipline of the Balance of Payments," *Journal of Finance*, May 1961, p. 184).

private long-term foreign investment such as the United States has experienced. The views of different countries about the amount of foreign economic aid or military expenditure which they are willing to undertake seem to be related in some crude way to their national income and not at all to the size of their foreign trade. The amount of capital which private investors place abroad is subject to many influences, but may be likely to vary from one investing country to another more according to the size of their national incomes and savings than according to the size of their foreign trade. Balance-of-payments deficits arising in these ways may therefore require relatively greater adjustments in a country's domestic economy and foreign trade when that trade is small than when it is large in relation to its total production.[9]

This difference would be of less consequence if wages and prices were flexible, as assumed in the classical theory of international trade, so that a moderately restrictive monetary policy might be counted upon to reduce prices relative to those of other countries, and thereby assist in the adjustment of the trade balance. In the United States and most other industrial countries, however, wages and prices have become relatively inflexible on the down side. Under these conditions, a contractionary policy aimed at adjusting the trade balance[10] would have to operate mainly through its effects on real income and employment, at least until the point is reached where wages and prices also begin to yield. If, therefore, balance-of-payments adjustment were to be pursued in this way, the amount of reduction required in real income and employment could be relatively great in the United States, com-

---

[9] There would, of course, be no reason a priori to expect such a difference in the case of balance-of-payments deficits arising in other ways, such as disturbances originating in the trade sector.

[10] A contractionary policy pursued through the tightening of credit would tend to reduce the outflow of capital into fixed-yield securities but to enhance the attractiveness of direct investment in countries where expansion is continuing, and would not, in itself, affect the size of foreign economic assistance and military expenditures.

pared with other countries, precisely for the reason that foreign trade is so small a part of its whole economy.[11]

It may therefore be that the country with the smallest involvement in international trade, measured in relation to its total economy, is more circumscribed than most in the choice of domestic policies open to it for making external adjustments. The limitations considered, it may be noted, are intrinsic to the world economic structure as it exists today. They are additional to those which can arise because, in a large, inward-oriented continental economy such as the United States, public attitudes are less disposed toward making adjustments needed for balance-of-payments purposes than in smaller countries more closely integrated into international trade.

LIMITATIONS ON EXCHANGE RATE POLICY

Given the special constraints to which the United States is subject in the use of deflation, one may ask if it does not then need to rely more on the other principal means of balance-of-payments adjustment to which countries have resorted—that is, a change in the foreign exchange value of the currency. This could mean either a devaluation of the dollar to a new parity relation with other currencies or a shift to a variable rate of exchange—alternatives which need to be sharply distinguished.

[11] More rigorously formulated, if a reduction of imports via a contraction of income is assumed to be the only means of adjusting to a balance-of-payments deficit, a deficit equal to a given percentage of gross national product will require a much sharper contraction in a country with a low import ratio, such as the United States, than in one with a high ratio typical of European countries. The difference can be illustrated as follows on the assumptions that, in both countries, prices are completely inflexible downward, that the income elasticity of demand for imports is unity, and that the balance-of-payments deficit is 1 per cent of gross national product:

	United States	Typical European Country
Imports as percentage of GNP	5	20
B/p deficit as percentage of GNP	1	1
Percentage contraction required in GNP to produce needed reduction in imports	20	5

It may be held that, here also, these options are less available to the United States than to countries playing a smaller role in international trade and finance. This is partly, to be sure, a matter of maintaining its political prestige in world affairs and partly a more specific question of its responsibilities and commitments toward those who have placed and kept their funds here. Viewed more pragmatically, there is the further consideration that a change in the exchange value of the leading reserve currency could leave a heritage of uncertainty and distrust such as to make all currencies henceforth more vulnerable to speculative attack in time of strain and to erode the basis for the operation of an international monetary system relying on market forces as distinguished from direct controls.

These objections would have less force if it were clear that the United States is, in the language of the International Monetary Fund, in "fundamental disequilibrium"[12] and that, as the appropriate remedy, it must sharply reduce its costs in relation to those of its competitors. In such cases, the quick surgery of devaluation, despite its damaging aftereffects, may be preferable to a prolonged compression of domestic demand in the effort to force down costs and prices.[13] In consideration of the elements of strength in the United States balance of payments observed in Chapter III, it would be difficult to maintain that the United States is today confronted with such a choice. Nor does the collective judgment of the market place appear to point to such a

---

[12] Article IV, Section 5, of the Articles of Agreement.

[13] Under the assumptions stated, the fixing of a new foreign exchange parity for the dollar would nevertheless appear to present exceptional difficulties and risks. The selection of a suitable par value for any currency inevitably involves a good deal of subjective judgment with regard to relative prices and other still more imponderable factors. The operation is complicated by the possibility that the extent of devaluation which would be appropriate for the short run may prove excessive after the full effects are registered. A small country can, however, afford to allow some margin for error, to be corrected by subsequent increases in its price level, without thereby imposing intolerable burdens on the currencies of other countries. This may even be true of a country as important as France, though it would now seem that the successive devaluations of its currency since the end of the war (the last of which was by 15 per cent at the end of 1958) may have given it an undue competitive advantage over other countries until and unless French costs and prices rise more than they have so far (see Tables 8-12, Chapter III). The United States could scarcely allow any such margin for error without imperiling the position of other currencies, yet a change too small to be accepted as definitive would only invite still more speculation against the dollar.

dilemma, given the fact that, on balance, foreign commercial banks, business concerns, and other private holders have substantially increased their reported liquid dollar assets here since the end of 1957.[14] It is also a measure of foreign confidence in the dollar that Europeans have continued to be the principal purchasers of European loan issues— denominated in dollars—floated in the United States capital market.

Looked at from the other side, it would be hard to identify any major foreign country, apart from France, which still appears to be in a state of persistent balance-of-payments surplus.[15] Moreover, as seen

[14] Reported U.S. liquid liabilities to foreign commercial banks and other private holders (as given in International Monetary Fund, *International Financial Statistics,* January 1963, pp. 272-273) rose from $5.7 billion at the end of 1957 to $7.5 billion at the end of June 1960, fell to $6.9 billion at the end of March 1961, rose to $8.4 billion a year later, and were again at the latter level at the end of October 1962. A considerable element of uncertainty is, however, introduced into these figures by the fact, noted in Chapter II, p. 18, that some foreign central banks are known to hold dollar funds through the intermediary of foreign commercial banks.

It is also of interest to note the behavior of U.S. short-term claims payable in major foreign currencies as reported by banks and nonfinancial concerns in the United States. These claims, though small in relation to reported U.S. short-term claims on other countries payable in dollars, rose by some $450 million between the end of March 1960 and the end of March 1961 (i.e., the period when foreign private funds here were being drawn down) to reach a total at the latter date of close to $800 million, after which they declined to about $570 million at the end of June 1962 (*Survey of Current Business,* September 1962, p. 13).

[15] France increased its reserves of gold and convertible currencies by $780 million during January-November 1962, compared with an increase of $870 million during the whole of 1961, and paid off $686 million of external debt during the full year 1962, compared with $375 million in 1961 (International Monetary Fund, *International Financial News Survey,* November 23, 1962, p. 375, *The New York Times,* December 5, 1962, and *The Christian Science Monitor,* January 16, 1963).

With reference to developments during 1961, the Bank for International Settlements commented: "The rise of prices in France over the past year gives a good illustration of the process of creeping inflation as it takes place in a full-employment economy." After reviewing changes in the internal and external position of France, however, the BIS concluded that "a sizable external surplus will persist and that ways should be sought to lessen its international impact as well as to minimise the tendency towards inflation that it can have at home" (*Thirty-Second Annual Report,* June 1962, pp. 9, 30).

in Chapter III, upward pressures on costs and prices in other industrial countries seem to be pervasive. There is, in fact, good reason to doubt that, even if it were disposed to do so, the United States could devalue the dollar without virtually all other currencies following along, some perhaps going even further, and hence with no benefit to its international competitive position as the end result of the exercise.[16]

A general devaluation of all currencies would have the result of raising the value of existing holdings of gold, both official and private, and of stimulating new gold production. Such a result is advocated by some as a means of increasing international liquidity, and by some others as part of a program for restoring the international gold standard along nineteenth-century lines and eliminating the use of dollars and sterling as international reserve media. Quite apart from the various questions which may be raised regarding these objectives, it is difficult to see how the operation could be carried through, on a jointly agreed basis, without provoking a gold panic in the process and without increasing private propensities to hoard gold in time of, or in anticipation of, future strains in international payments.[17] It is estimated that during

---

[16] This does not mean, of course, that the dollar or other currencies could not succumb to speculative pressures, but only that the final result might be no more rational or defensible than the present position.

[17] For arguments in favor of an increase in the price of gold, see Sir Roy Harrod, "The Dollar Problem and the Gold Question," in Harris (ed.), *The Dollar in Crisis,* and Michael A. Heilperin, "The Case for Going Back to Gold," *Fortune,* September 1962.

Heilperin's presentation has the advantage of being fairly precise as to the steps he envisages, though his precision may also suggest to the reader how difficult it would be to carry them out. "Phase I" would be an agreement by the countries of the Atlantic Community, including the United States, "to pay balance-of-payments deficits in gold and gold only" and not to accumulate further reserves of dollars and sterling. "Phase II" would consist of "three separate but simultaneous moves," to wit: (1) "a decision by the United States to pay off in gold all short-term dollar obligations held by foreigners"—to be carried out, however, only after taking the third step listed below, (2) an agreement by countries of the Atlantic Community "to make all their currencies fully convertible into gold" for both foreign and domestic claimants, (3) joint action "to double the price of gold in all currencies."

How a program aimed at doubling the price of gold could be undertaken, or even seriously considered, without at once precipitating a massive run on the gold stocks of the United States and other countries is not clear. Heilperin says that "this will require considerable ingenuity and skill." That may be an understatement. It would seem to require not only exceptional speed and secrecy in

the period 1946 to 1961, at least $7.5 billion was added to private gold hoards, or something more than the increase in monetary gold stocks from new supplies during the same period.[18] If speculation in gold, for some years an unprofitable investment for many, were now to be well rewarded with a general increase in its price, one may wonder how much gold would henceforth disappear into private hoards. Perhaps the upshot would be that gold would be less available, at the same time that national currencies would have been rendered less acceptable, as reserve media. It would be ironical if a rise in the price of gold, by increasing hoarding propensities, were to end by necessitating the demonetization of gold.

If it were clear that the dollar is overvalued, a switch to a regime of variable exchange rates for the dollar—with no fixed ties to gold—might reduce the risk which a new devaluation would entail of increasing the vulnerability of the international monetary system to gold speculation. Proponents of such a regime, finding new support for their views in present balance-of-payments difficulties,[19] also consider that, in a longer perspective, a variable rate would have the advantage of permitting smooth and more or less automatic adjustments to such new balance-of-payments disturbances as may arise and of providing a

---

composing differences of views among national monetary authorities but also an extraordinary, and perhaps improbable, willingness on the part of countries holding dollars and sterling as reserves to abstain from converting them into gold at the beginning rather than at the end of the exercise.

[18] See Oscar L. Altman, "Quelques Aspects du Problème de l'Or," *Cahiers de l'Institut de Science Economique Appliquée*, Series R, No. 7, October 1962. Altman states that his estimate is based upon totals for free-world gold production of $15.9 billion, Soviet gold sales of $1.6 billion, industrial and artistic uses of $2.7 billion, and additions of $7 billion to world monetary gold stocks.

During the first nine months of 1962, additions to free-world monetary gold stocks were only some $200 million (*International Financial Statistics*, December 1962, pp. 18, 32), or about one-fifth of probable gold production outside the Soviet area during that period.

[19] See, for example, the paper "Objectives, Monetary Standards, and Potentialities" by Harry G. Johnson presented at the Conference on Monetary Economics, April 13 and 14, 1962, sponsored by the Universities-National Bureau Committee for Economic Research, and also the contributions "Long-Run Factors in United States Payments Disequilibrium" by Jaroslav Vanek and "The Dollar and the Mark" by Egon Sohmen in Harris (ed.), *The Dollar in Crisis*, pp. 165-182 and 183-200.

better basis for the conduct of domestic economic policy.[20] In this view of the matter, a variable rate is not necessarily an unstable rate: temporary disparities between supply and demand in the foreign exchange market would be evened out by private anticipations or by official intervention. More basic changes in the flows of trade and capital would, however, shift exchange rates enough to restore balance by altering relative costs and prices among countries and spare them from having to try to make balance-of-payments adjustments by operating on the general level of domestic economic activity and prices. The working of the price mechanism, inhibited internally in various ways, would thus be restored in the foreign exchange market.

At its hypothetical best, flexibility of exchange rates would seem to be peculiarly suited to the conditions of this large economy in which, as has been seen, external transactions play a relatively smaller but sometimes more awkward role than in other countries more dependent on international trade. Strong doubts have, however, been raised as to whether the theoretical advantages of such a regime would not be outweighed by its disadvantages in practice—whether, in fact, speculation in the foreign exchange market would be stabilizing or destabilizing, or, if stabilizing, whether or not fluctuations in rates would remain within tolerable limits; whether uncertainty about the future course of exchange rates would handicap foreign trade or could be offset by the further development of the forward market and other types of hedging; whether or not uncertainty about exchange rates over the longer run would inhibit international investment; whether or not exchange rate variations, actual or anticipated, would be such as to provoke new restrictions on international trade and create new impediments to international economic cooperation.

These doubts, which are of general applicability to variable exchange rate regimes, have special force in relation to the international position of the United States and the role of the dollar in international finance. Given the large foreign accumulations of dollar balances and

[20] With respect to domestic economic policy, the proponents of a variable exchange rate seem to divide into two rather sharply opposed groups—those who believe that such a regime, even more than a fixed rate, would impose a desirable discipline on domestic policies lest the rate fluctuate unduly, and those who value such a regime because it would allow, even if at the risk of continuing depreciation of the currency, greater freedom from external constraint in the pursuit of domestic objectives. Clearly, therefore, what is desired by its proponents is not a variable rate alone but a variable rate along with a commitment to a particular constellation of domestic economic policies, a rather different one in the two cases.

the increased readiness of domestic holders of liquid assets to place their funds abroad, the prospect that the exodus of capital could become self-aggravating, with cumulatively depressive effects on the exchange value of the dollar, cannot be lightly dismissed. Such a risk would always be present in greater or lesser degree but would be especially serious at the time of transition from a fixed to a variable rate—all the more so if the currency had already become subject to question. It may be pleasant to suppose that, after a dip of only a few points, confidence would grow that a new equilibrium level had been reached and that private operations in foreign exchange would then become stabilizing. Little encouragement for such an expectation is provided by the experience of Canada prior to the decision in May 1962 to establish a new par value. Its difficulties, first in depressing the Canadian dollar from a level deemed too high and then in preventing the fall, once it had started, from becoming excessive, show how drastically private evaluations and behavior can shift.

To try to foresee the ultimate consequences of shifting to a floating dollar would be guesswork. One cannot, however, ignore the danger that many countries might reinstate direct controls over trade and payments. Memories of exchange depreciation in the 1930's, with suspicions of beggar-my-neighbor motivations, may still be fresh enough to ensure resurrection of the defensive measures employed at that time. Few countries would be likely to leave their home markets open to the play of a dollar determined by market forces, unless indeed confidence in the stabilizing effect of private speculation were shared in advance by foreign monetary authorities and confirmed in the event.

It is not the direct effect on the United States economy of a renewal of foreign restrictions on its exports that is most to be feared—the amount of damage that could be inflicted in this way on a country whose foreign trade is so small a part of its total production is limited. What may be feared is rather the effect on other countries more dependent on access to foreign markets and less able to defend themselves against a new wave of economic nationalism or regionalism, and, beyond that, the disruption of good relations in general among the countries with which we are most closely associated. A variable rate of exchange might be more appropriate to a world in which the United States had to retrench politically and militarily as well as economically—a "Fortress America" concept of this country's international posture—than to one in which it aspires to greater unity with its allies and to the creation of conditions favorable to the development of the weaker countries.

To sum up, given the complexity of the issues and the paucity of relevant historical experience, one can scarcely be dogmatic in asserting either the advantages or the disadvantages of a variable rate of exchange compared with those of a fixed rate. Each may be said to offer certain benefits and to entail certain risks and sacrifices. Where the balance of advantage lies for the United States goes beyond purely national economic considerations and involves a weighing of this country's basic objectives in the world economy. Circumstances could arise under which, from the standpoint of our domestic interests, a flexible rate would seem clearly preferable to trying to maintain exchange rate stability *coûte que coûte*. This might be so if the disturbances to which the balance of payments may be subjected were such as to impose burdens of adjustment and constraints on policy greater than the economy could reasonably be expected to bear, or if our capacity to adjust to more moderate disturbances proved inadequate because of inability to agree upon and apply such means of adjustment as are available to us. The present analysis suggests that, following the substantial increase in balance-of-payments burdens and other quite severe disturbances during the past decade, adjustments are in fact being made in relative prices and trade flows, and that there may be merit in trying to improve the functioning of the present system rather than reaching out for the uncertain benefits of a radically different regime.

3. *Possibilities of Improving Processes of Adjustment*

It seems to be standard practice to accompany measures or proposals for increasing international liquidity with strictures that no such schemes will work if countries run large and persistent deficits or surpluses in their balances of payments and that, accordingly, ways of correcting maladjustments need to be improved. A sense of realism compels one to recognize that the ways of doing so are fairly limited in number and in speed of operation, if both deflation and changes in exchange rates are ruled out as particularly inappropriate means of adjustment for the United States to employ. It is therefore all the more necessary to consider what possibilities there are and to be able to avail ourselves of them.

REMNANTS OF A GENERAL MECHANISM OF ADJUSTMENT

The exclusion of deflation does not mean that no possibility remains of achieving adjustments in relative prices between the United States and other countries. In the course of the last several years, various American commentators have suggested, sometimes with a slightly apologetic tone, that the United States balance of payments would be helped by a little wage and price inflation in the main surplus countries. As noted in Chapter III, this hope is not being disappointed—not as the result of policies aimed at this objective but also not without some causal influence stemming from balance-of-payments surpluses. It is sometimes overlooked that these surpluses have been among the potent sources of expansion in the countries of Continental Europe and have thereby contributed to the adjustments needed to restore balance. The conclusion to be drawn from this experience may be, not that adjustment processes are absent, but that they require time to produce their effects. Reciprocal action on the side of the United States would consist of keeping wage increases smaller than productivity gains and of distributing part of these gains through reductions in the general level of prices. This result would be of special importance in manufactures, both because of their role in international competition and because of the more rapid increase in productivity in manufacturing than in most other sectors. So far, however, official policy expressions do not seem to aspire to more than price stability.

The possibility of producing a "differential trend" in prices in this way was described, in the Annual Report of the Netherlands Bank for 1960, as "the only policy which remains available as a means of restoring equilibrium."[21] In its report for 1961 the Netherlands Bank returned to this theme with the following comment:

Reasonable progress was also achieved in connection with the differential movement in production costs, although it must unfortunately be stated that the contribution towards restoring equilibrium in that sphere came rather onesidedly from Europe alone. In Europe during the year under report the course of wages and per capita productivity everywhere raised the labour costs per unit of industrial product, while in the United States, partly thanks to improving economic activity, the costs of labour remained virtually unaltered.

This process incidentally shows the error of propounding, on both sides of the Ocean alike, the principle that labour costs ought to rise in proportion to the

[21] P. 16.

average increase of per capita productivity. However right this formula may be if one disregards the requirements of international equilibrium, and pays attention only to the desirability of maintaining internal price stability, its realisation would definitely hinder the differential cost movements which are a necessary precondition for restoring external equilibrium while maintaining fixed rates of exchange. In countries with a structural balance of payments deficit the costs of labour per unit of product must fall so that, through a certain lowering of prices, their ability to compete on the world market may be improved. Countries with a structural surplus on their balance of payments must on the other hand—if they wish to preserve parity of exchange with foreign countries—accept a certain rise in nominal wages above that of productivity, so that they too may thus contribute towards restoring international equilibrium.[22]

It is not yet clear how much can be accomplished along these lines by way of maintaining a general mechanism of adjustment, especially if the adjustment has to come solely by way of price increases on the part of countries in balance-of-payments surplus. It is true that moderate inflation is likely to be a more feasible course than deflation as far as popular reactions are concerned. But it is also true that the authorities in countries gaining reserves are under less pressure to correct their positions than those in countries losing reserves, and the first may choose instead to resist expansion in the interest of price stability. On another occasion, moreover, countries with surpluses may not be experiencing as much tension in the labor market as they have in recent years, and rates of wage increases may have become adjusted to a more moderate growth of productivity.[23] Under these circumstances, the possibility of achieving a "differential trend" may depend heavily in the future on the development of a clearer consensus of views in the United States with regard to ways of adjusting wage and price changes to meet the needs of the external situation.

Though it is apparently never explicitly included in the theory of international trade as part of the classical mechanism of adjustment, it may be appropriate to refer here to the concept of "competitive

[22] De Nederlandsche Bank N.V., *Report for the Year 1961,* May 1962, p. 20.

[23] The rapid wage increases in European countries during the past year or so may represent a carry-forward of the momentum gradually built up during the preceding period of rapid growth in productivity.

response," already mentioned in Chapter III.[24] This is the thought that, along with the general price and income effects which may be associated with balance-of-payments disturbances and adjustments, another feature of the adjustment mechanism is the effort of producers to retain or recapture markets in the face of increased foreign competition. It is possible that, in a more searching inquiry into the nature of the adjustments made by the United States in recent years, some weight will need to be attached to this factor. The introduction of the compact car by Detroit could by now be regarded as a classic example of competitive response. Another is the strengthening of the United States position in the production of semiconductors in response to Japanese competition. More generally, it appears that intensive cost-cutting programs have been undertaken in important sections of American industry in order to compete more effectively at home and abroad. Producers may, of course, be only partially successful and turn to other lines less beneficial to the balance of payments, or put up with idle capacity. In general, policies by government, business, and labor that increase the capacity of industry to adjust and innovate will tend also to strengthen its ability to respond competitively to disturbances in foreign trade.

OTHER MEANS OF PROMOTING ADJUSTMENTS

If what remains of a general mechanism of adjustment, including the effects of policies aimed at influencing the general level of costs and prices, proves inadequate to the task, the only other processes of adjustment are the specific steps which the Government may be able to take with regard to particular items of expenditure and receipt in the balance of payments. As discussed in Chapter III, the possibilities for direct action have been considerable in recent years, especially with regard to the Government's own large foreign operations and in the area of export promotion. Except for the prepayment of foreign debt and an increase in military receipts, the results actually registered so far appear to have been modest. The fact that time is required for action to become effective, taken in conjunction with the improvement nevertheless registered in the balance on basic transactions, may

24 See also Hal B. Lary, "Disturbances and Adjustments in Recent U.S. Balance of Payments Experience," *American Economic Review*, May 1961, p. 417.

be favorable in its implications for the further strengthening of the balance.

If, however, one considers the question of improving adjustment processes to meet future contingencies, it cannot be taken for granted that similar opportunities for direct action on individual items will always be present. Most of the measures which have been taken come up against more or less clearly foreseeable limits in what they can contribute—for instance, the extent to which foreign aid can be tied, or the volume of sales of military equipment that can be made to other countries on a continuing basis, or the amount of foreign debt that might be prepaid. The promotion of exports may be an exception: in a country in which so few engage in foreign trade, there may always be possibilities of arousing the interest of additional producers in export markets. Some ingenuity may also need to be employed in developing tax or other incentives to export in order to equalize competitive conditions with other industrial countries.[25]

4. *The Prevention of Disruptive Movements of Liquid Capital*

RECONCILIATION OF INTERNAL AND EXTERNAL OBJECTIVES

The analysis so far in this paper suggests that basic adjustments can be made, and apparently are being made, in the balance of pay-

---

[25] Direct subsidies to exports would be difficult to reconcile with the anti-dumping provisions of the GATT. A number of European countries accomplish the same purpose by refunding turnover taxes to exporters, enabling them to quote lower prices to the export market than those charged to domestic customers. With the minor exception of excise taxes, taxes in the United States do not readily lend themselves to reimbursement in the same way. This might become more feasible if there were, as some would prefer on broader grounds, a shift in this country from the corporate income tax to a tax on value added. Other possibilities for providing export incentives through the tax system could be explored—for instance, the allowance of tax credits for expenses incurred in developing export outlets.

Perhaps a still more desirable, if unlikely, alternative to such new departures by the United States would be for European countries to dispense with their special tax incentives to exports. Even if these incentives are not regarded as dumping, they seem to make no more sense internally than internationally at a time when European resources available for home use are severely strained.

ments. But, with reference to the adjustments still needed or those which may be required to meet new strains, the analysis also points to the conclusion that the processes of adjustment are severely limited in the choices open to the United States and that they are likely to be slow and cumbersome in producing the desired effects.

These circumstances make it all the more essential, though at times also more difficult, to be able to keep movements of liquid capital from assuming disruptive proportions.[26] If it were considered that the monetary authorities could not, in the future, hold this flow well beneath the levels of 1960 and 1961, then neither would there be any strong assurance that they could keep it from rising to still higher levels.

In brief, the commitment to a stable rate of exchange presupposes that the United States stands ready to apply measures to keep from being drained of its reserves by excessive outflows of liquid funds. The dollar could scarcely be successfully defended over the long run if the lines of action available to the United States were so circumscribed that it could not operate quickly and effectively either on those sectors of the balance of payments which are not sensitive to monetary policy or on those which are. In the deployment of its economic policies, the United States could scarcely expect to operate with the freedom associated, in the minds of some of its advocates, with variable rates of exchange without sooner or later finding the dollar on such a basis.

It is only in the last few years that the United States has had to face these limitations. As expressed in the Annual Report for 1961 of the Federal Reserve Bank of New York, "In the early years of the Federal Reserve System, formulation of monetary policy was in many ways and for a variety of reasons oriented predominantly toward domestic problems," and "international monetary relations remained largely peripheral."[27] After the Second World War, the United States was

---

[26] As noted in Chapter II, p. 15, and more fully discussed in Appendix A, the concept of "liquid" capital employed here is broader than recorded "short-term" capital (or that part of the latter going into liquid assets) and refers more generally to all kinds of capital movements which, at the time of transfer, may be considered as relatively sensitive to monetary influences and policies. The concept would thus include those unidentified capital flows which may be deduced from the behavior of the "unrecorded transactions" (errors and omissions) and perhaps some types of "long-term" capital movements, such as new foreign bond flotations and transfers of funds between American companies and their foreign subsidiaries.

[27] P. 6.

spared the usual balance-of-payments constraints as long as other countries desired to accumulate assets in its currency for foreign exchange reserves, working balances or other purposes,[28] and as long as the inconvertibility of other currencies posed an effective barrier to major outflows of United States private funds. These conditions provided a shield behind which the development of the theory and practice of economic policy could be concentrated on domestic problems and objectives.[29]

These conditions also meant that the United States could rely more heavily on monetary policy than was possible in other countries whose exposed positions required them to adapt their credit and interest rate policies to their external circumstances and to develop other instruments, especially in the area of fiscal policy, to serve their domestic objectives.

To quote again the Federal Reserve Bank of New York, "It is only now, more than fifteen years after the war, that the full scope of the required changes in the foreign economic and financial relations of the United States begins to emerge. The idealistic concept of One World has become the hard reality of world-wide competition and capital movements. . . . The hard facts of recent balance-of-payments developments, in the context of the international role of the dollar, have revised the basic framework for monetary policy in the United States."[30]

As one of the major consequences of these changes, it seems clear that the United States will be less able to rely on monetary ease as the preferred means for combating recession, and that the only broad alternative or complement to monetary policy is fiscal policy. Indeed, even before the new external constraint developed, the beneficial effects of the "built-in stabilizers" in the federal budget and the need

[28] Termed "deficit without tears" by Jacques Rueff, *Fortune*, July 1961, p. 127.

[29] It is an interesting commentary on the domestic orientation of economic policy that the Employment Act of 1946 made no reference to external economic relations. This omission doubtless reflected an implicit assumption, not unreasonable at the time, that outside developments could not impose any significant constraint on the formulation of economic policies with regard to domestic employment.

[30] Annual Report, 1961, pp. 6, 7.

for greater flexibility in fiscal policy were being stressed.[31] In practice, however, only limited progress has been made in developing the necessary fiscal tools and the skills needed in their use, in harmonizing differences of views between those favoring tax reductions and those favoring increases in expenditures as a means of countering recession and stimulating production and employment, and in studying the economic effects which could be produced by changes in the structure, as well as levels, of government receipts and expenditures.

The view is sometimes expressed that an expansionary fiscal policy to stimulate the domestic economy would be nullified in its effects if it were also necessary to raise interest rates in order to curb the outflow of capital.[32] This argument appears to be based on the assumption that an increase in interest rates sufficient to reduce the outflow of capital could be achieved only by tightening credit to the point where the effects of fiscal expansion would be fully offset. It is difficult to see why this should be so. An expansion induced exclusively by an increase in expenditure in the private sector would ordinarily give

[31] "Fiscal policy is a less flexible instrument than either monetary or debt management policy for keeping the economy on a narrow path that separates inflation from recession. But Federal operations are now so large a factor in our economy that their variations, whether on the revenue or expenditure side, are bound to have a significant impact on our economy. The deliberate use of fiscal policy, in the interest of maintaining a sound economy, bears great promise for the future, and the actions taken in 1953 reflected this concern" (*Economic Report of the President,* January 1954, p. 52).

[32] An argument along this line is developed by J. Herbert Furth in "The Dilemma of United States Monetary Policy," *Pennsylvania Business Survey,* May 1962.

A vigorous exposition of the view that "fiscal policy . . . should make the necessary adaptation" is given in Part I, pp. 3-36, of the *Thirty-Second Annual Report* (for year ended March 31, 1962) of the Bank for International Settlements. The report comments that "The United States is the only country that has not put major emphasis in monetary measures on external requirements, which has been seen to be necessary since the return to convertibility" (p. 23). It further states: "There is ample European experience to show that the possible internal restraint of a tighter monetary policy can be alleviated by fiscal and other policy means. Over the longer run the United States, as a great financial centre, should be an exporter of capital and have an interest rate structure that facilitates the investment of its excess savings overseas. Given its other burdens, however, the United States has no excess savings on external account at the moment, and it is not appropriate that the combination of policies followed on both sides of the Atlantic should be encouraging a net flow of capital towards Europe which has to be financed by U.S. gold losses and the piling-up of short-term dollar liabilities" (p. 24).

rise to some increase in interest rates, without the expansion thereby being brought to a halt. Equally, it should be possible to initiate or continue an expansion by fiscal policy and to support the expansion by an increase in the money supply, but yet not so freely as to prevent some hardening of interest rates when this is needed in the interest of internal or external stability. The crucial question may be one of sequence and timing—that is, to avoid a premature increase in interest rates, but to allow them to edge up as the demand for credit strengthens.[33]

Possibilities of Enlarging the Scope for Monetary Policy

The question may also be considered whether, despite the new exposure of the American money market to international forces, means can be developed to provide more freedom of action for monetary policy. Or, as put by the chairman of the Council of Economic Advisors, "what are the possibilities of its serving two masters—domestic and international objectives—at once?"[34]

The effort to resolve this dilemma and, more specifically, to reduce the risk of capital outflows of a sudden and disruptive nature has produced greater innovation in this than in perhaps any other area of

[33] Study also needs to be given to the view that, if tax rates are such that they would yield unduly high revenues in relation to expenditures under full employment conditions, they will exert a damping effect on the economy sufficient to prevent the attainment either of full employment or of a budget surplus. See testimony by Charles L. Schultze before the Joint Economic Committee (*Current Economic Situation and Outlook*, December 7 and 8, 1960, pp. 114-122). See also Robert Solomon, "The Full Employment Budget Surplus as an Analytical Concept," paper presented at the annual meeting of the American Statistical Association, Minneapolis, September 8, 1962.

Herbert Stein related this argument to monetary policy and interest rates in his testimony before the Joint Economic Committee on February 10, 1961 (*January 1961 Economic Report of the President and the Economic Situation and Outlook*, p. 213): "The attempt to achieve high employment in the face of a budget that would yield very large surpluses at high employment requires rapid monetary expansion to offset the depressing effect of the budget. This means low interest rates, and, unless other countries are following a similar policy, this is likely to cause an outflow of capital and balance-of-payments difficulties."

[34] *International Payments Imbalances and Need for Strengthening International Financial Arrangements*, Hearings before the Subcommittee on International Exchange and Payments of the Joint Economic Committee, Washington, June 1961, p. 50.

economic policy during the past two years, including:[35]

Active intervention in the foreign exchange market by the Treasury and Federal Reserve, in cooperation with foreign central banks, to combat temporary disturbances. These operations began in March 1961 with forward sales of German marks in order to reduce the discount on the forward dollar at a time of strong speculation on a further upward revaluation of the mark. The increase in the amount of forward cover available served to encourage the holding of dollars, to reduce demands for spot conversions into marks, and to calm speculative unrest. The Treasury's forward mark commitments reached a peak of $340 million in mid-June 1961 and then declined rapidly. Operations have subsequently been made in other currencies, especially Swiss francs, guilders, and lire.

Bilateral reciprocal credit arrangements, or swap facilities, negotiated by the Federal Reserve, starting in March 1962, with foreign central banks for the exchange of currencies for use in currency stabilization operations. These facilities, though extended for a short period such as three or six months, are renewable by mutual agreement. Through October 1961, arrangements had been made with nine foreign central banks and with the Bank for International Settlements for a total of $800 million. The largest was a $250 million swap with the Bank of Canada in June 1962 as part of a program of international support for the Canadian dollar at its new par value.[36]

Negotiation of a multilateral agreement with nine other leading financial and trading countries providing "supplementary resources" up to a total of $6 billion (or $4 billion by countries other than the United States) for mutual financial assistance through the International Monetary Fund, to be used

---

[35] The foreign exchange operations of the Treasury and Federal Reserve during the period March 1961–August 1962 are reviewed in a "joint interim report," prepared by Charles A. Coombs, in the *Monthly Review* of the Federal Reserve Bank of New York, October 1962. Other details are given in various articles and addresses by Treasury officials, including in particular the addresses by Secretary Dillon on September 19, 1962, at the annual meeting of the International Monetary Fund and by Under Secretary Roosa on May 17, 1962, at the Monetary Conference of the American Bankers Association in Rome, Italy, and Under Secretary Roosa's testimony on December 13, 1962, before the Subcommittee on International Exchange and Payments of the Joint Economic Committee (Treasury press releases).

[36] Other elements in the program were a $400 million stand-by credit to the Canadian Government by the U.S. Export-Import Bank, a $100 million credit to the Bank of Canada by the Bank of England, and a Canadian drawing of $300 million on the International Monetary Fund. The Canadian borrowings from the Federal Reserve and the Bank of England were fully repaid during the fourth quarter of 1962, leaving the IMF drawing still outstanding at the end of the year.

particularly in the event of massive shifts of funds from one country to others.[37]

Outright acquisitions of foreign currencies (without provision for gold or currency value guarantee) to be held alongside gold as part of the monetary reserves of the United States.

Borrowings of foreign currencies by the United States against the issuance of obligations, of various maturities, denominated in the currencies concerned.

Cooperation among the monetary authorities of the leading countries in handling transactions on the London gold market, with the aim of preventing speculative runs on currencies which could be triggered by excessive fluctuations in the price of gold and of allowing the price to vary only enough to make speculation costly.

Intensified international consultation among monetary authorities through the Bank for International Settlements and the Organization for Economic Cooperation and Development.

These innovations provide the monetary authorities with powerful resources and instruments, fully adequate no doubt to ensure against a sudden speculative attack on one or another of the major currencies.[38] It may be doubted, however, that they would permit the United States again to hold its interest rates appreciably below those of the principal foreign financial markets for an extended period, at least until the balance of payments is much stronger.

If still greater scope is desired for an independent monetary policy, the American money market itself may have to be divorced in some measure from foreign money markets. One way would be by differentiating the rates applicable in the domestic and in the foreign sectors of the American market—for example, by developing additional special

[37] Further comments on this agreement are given below, pp. 131-132.

[38] Prominent by its absence from the measures taken is the idea sometimes advocated of guaranteeing foreign official holders of dollar balances against loss in terms of gold so as to enhance their willingness to keep funds here. Under Secretary Roosa has argued strongly against such a guarantee on the ground that, if it were offered as a basis for the agreement of other countries to hold dollars, they would then be in a position to exact, sooner or later, conditions regarding the conduct of our economic and financial policies along lines which they might consider necessary to make the guarantee trustworthy (Robert V. Roosa, "Assuring the Free World's Liquidity," Federal Reserve Bank of Philadelphia, *Business Review* supplement, September 1962. It may be unrealistic, moreover, to suppose that the United States would be willing to give foreign holders of dollars an advantage not enjoyed by its own citizens or by the people and government of the United States with respect to their own investments in other countries. One may also wonder whether the creation of a distinction between guaranteed dollars and other dollars might not make the latter even more susceptible of transfer abroad in time of strain when the guarantee might have been expected to prove useful.

credit instruments paying higher rates to foreign than to American lenders and by employing taxes or other means so as to charge higher rates to foreign than to American borrowers. A still sharper separation could be created by the establishment of limits, which could vary according to changing circumstances, on the amount of bankers' acceptances or other credits extended to foreigners and on short-term placements abroad by banks and business firms. While it is difficult to imagine that a comprehensive system of exchange controls could be successfully applied in this country under peacetime conditions, selective restraints on the money market of the nature mentioned might be more feasible and sufficient to prevent capital flows from again assuming a self-aggravating character.

These possibilities become progressively less agreeable to contemplate and could be regarded as alternatives to be considered only in the event that other combinations of policies cannot be agreed upon or made effective. Official opinion in the United States makes a distinction, which may be easier to defend on grounds of feasibility than of strict logic, between special measures to attract foreign capital and special measures to deter the outflow of American capital. Thus it has not been averse to paying interest rates discriminating in favor of foreign official holdings of U.S. government securities and of time and savings deposits in U.S. banks to strengthen the inducement to hold reserves in dollars rather than gold, while allowing domestic rates to be kept at lower levels.[39] It has, on the other hand, opposed any kind of surcharge or administrative check on loans and credits to foreigners on the ground that such action "might handicap the functioning of a competitive, market economy."[40]

---

[39] Cf. the President's Message on Balance of Payments and Gold, February 6, 1961. That message directed the Secretary of the Treasury to use existing authority, when it seemed desirable, to issue securities at special rates of interest for holding by foreign governments or monetary authorities, and it also proposed legislation, passed in October 1962, enabling the United States banking authorities to establish separate maxima for interest rates on time deposits held by foreign governments or monetary authorities.

[40] Address by Under Secretary Roosa on September 25, 1962, at the annual convention of the American Bankers Association. Roosa also stated: "Our own money and capital markets are the most highly organized, most efficiently diversified, of any in the world. To try to impose controls over outward capital movements in any one sector of these markets—say bank loans—would only invite capital flight through many others."

It is relevant to note, if only in order to understand the distinctive nature of our -problems, that such direct methods are employed in some other countries enjoying a high reputation for the success of their economic and financial policies. Moreover, in countries whose banking systems comprise a very few large institutions with many branches, the monetary authorities are sometimes able to rely on informal contact and moral suasion to accomplish their objectives to an extent that would be difficult and perhaps even productive of adverse reactions in the United States with its dispersed banking system.[41] Similar differences may sometimes be noted with respect to other policies affecting foreign trade and investment—or the domestic economy, too, for that matter. The relatively high development of our competitive system composed of many individual units may make it more difficult than in more centralized economies to channel national efforts toward specific objectives. These distinguishing features of the American economy enhance the need for improving the instruments of general economic policy to provide more flexibility in making adjustments to a rapidly changing world economic environment.

[41] Switzerland is an interesting case in point, especially in view of the high esteem in which the Swiss franc is held. During the 1930's, when the outflow of capital from Switzerland began to make an excessive drain on monetary reserves, the Swiss National Bank concluded a gentlemen's agreement with the Swiss commercial banks whereby they agreed to limitations designed to hold the capital movement to a level consistent with the country's position. Later, a law was passed making the flotation of foreign loan issues subject to official approval. These instruments remain available for use, though recently Switzerland has had to contend with the opposite problem of capital inflows on such a scale as to threaten the creation of excessive liquidity.

In the light of Swiss experience and practice, it is interesting to note the following comments on U.S. capital outflows by the General Manager of the Swiss National Bank in an address given in Switzerland on October 20, 1962: "The Swiss monetary authorities have repeatedly pointed out to their American colleagues that, although this willingness to supply the world with capital is very generous and deserves gratitude, such generosity is hard to understand if capital exports endanger the U.S. balance of payments and its currency. In Europe, we tell them, capital exports are regarded as a valuable means of offsetting a surplus in the balance of payments. If the balance of payments of a European country were heavily in deficit, however, restrictions would be placed on capital exports. For the moment, though, such an idea is utterly rejected in the United States, as freedom of capital exports is thought to be one of the functions of a world currency. From our point of view, we should prefer equilibrium in the balance of payments and reduced capital exports, because we feel it to be important for confidence in the dollar to be restored as soon as possible."

None of the foregoing discussion of policy alternatives is to be regarded as implying the necessity for a particular policy or combination of policies at a particular time. The nature, vigor, and time of the action taken are questions of judgment to be decided in relation to a host of considerations, including the relative urgency of the domestic and the external situations, the trend and outlook in the basic items in the balance of payments, the state of the gold reserves, the purposes being served by capital movements, and the presence of any self-limiting or self-aggravating elements in these movements, including the state of public confidence. It may be more important to our objectives and ultimate success to persuade European countries to assume a larger share of the world's economic burdens and to make their money and capital markets more accessible to others than for us to impose more stringent or preclusive policies in this country. The question is, once again, whether or not such policies can be applied and made effective if the situation is judged to require it.

The problem of reconciling internal and external objectives may prove somewhat less difficult in the future than it has appeared recently. For one thing, the extraordinary scale on which American bank credit was extended to other countries during 1960 and 1961 may keep new credit extensions of this nature at a more moderate level for some time to come. Second, short-term interest rates declined during 1962 in the money markets of most European countries, and toward the end of the year were lower in several Continental European countries than in the United States, as measured by the yield on three-month Treasury bills. Third, the problem may be eased by the further development of techniques and cooperative measures to discourage or offset undesirable capital movements. Finally, the tendency for capital flows which occur in response to earnings differentials to provoke other more speculative flows through changes in public confidence may be weakened to the extent that, as discussed in Chapter III, further progress can be made in strengthening the balance on basic transactions.

5. *The Need of the United States for Large Reserves*

Resources, whether owned or borrowed, for financing balance-of-payments deficits relieve in some measure the conflict between internal and external objectives by allowing time for adjustments to be made. By the same token, they may have the disadvantage of permitting necessary adjustments to be unduly delayed. It may seem that there has been too much of the second and not enough of the first during the last several years. And yet, once it became clear that the United States was in serious balance-of-payments difficulty, one may ask whether its interest or that of other countries would have been better served if, for lack of means to finance the deficit, the United States had had to resort to such drastic means of closing the gap as import restrictions, devaluation, or a severe contraction of domestic economic activity and employment.[42]

This dilemma persists with the narrowing of the limits within which the United States can expect to finance a deficit, either now or in the event of future disturbances in its international payments. The compulsion to adhere to a closer balance can be regarded as a necessary and desirable manifestation of the "discipline of the balance of payments." But if the affirmation of this necessity is to be more than axiomatic, it should reflect a considered judgment as to the most feasible and acceptable ways of keeping deficits, should they recur, and the means of financing them in a realistic relationship to each other. Clearly, adjustment processes cannot be so ineffective as to call for unlimited financing. Nor, on the other hand, can the means of financing be so limited as to imply that miracles of speed and efficiency are expected of the available processes of adjustment.

DISTINCTIVE ASPECTS OF U.S. PAYMENTS POSITION

The problem is not merely how soon the present balance-of-payments deficit can be eliminated. The analysis of recent experience in earlier sections of this paper has pointed to some reasons for encouragement in this regard, including the basic competitive strength of the United States, evidences of improvement in its relative cost position

---

[42] Milder measures taken earlier in the 1950's and, in particular, a more effective resistance to inflation in the United States during the 1955-1957 period would doubtless have helped to ward off the large balance-of-payments deficits of later years and to strengthen the capacity of the United States to adjust to other changes which were occurring in the world economy. But it is more doubtful, once the gap opened as wide as it did in 1958, that corrective action could have greatly accelerated the adjustment without, in the language of the IMF, "resorting to measures destructive of national or international prospertity" (Article I(vi) of the Articles of Agreement of the International Monetary Fund).

during the last two or three years, and the various policy measures taken to redress the balance. But the experience also serves to show what strains can arise in a rapidly changing world economy and how slow adjustments to these strains may be. By way of recapitulation of some of the main elements in this experience, it may be suggested that the United States needs exceptionally large reserves or other possibilities of financing deficits because of:

> The risk that new disturbances may arise from changes in international trade and investment, including especially the agricultural and commercial policies of the Common Market countries.

> The risk also that disturbances of a political or military nature may occur, entailing increases in U.S. government expenditures abroad.

> Limitations on the means available to the United States for adjusting to disturbances in basic transactions and, it would appear, a greater sluggishness in making adjustments compared with countries whose economies are more closely geared to international trade.

> The role of the United States as an international reserve center, including the right of foreign monetary authorities to convert their dollar holdings into gold.

> The increased international mobility of private capital, American as well as foreign, and the risk that capital outflows may at times take on a speculative and self-aggravating character.

> The incompatibility with American traditions and institutions of the more direct methods sometimes employed in other countries to prevent capital movements from becoming excessive.

> The historical reliance of the United States on monetary policy as the preferred instrument for guiding the domestic economy and the consequent difficulty of subordinating monetary policy to balance-of-payments needs.

> The additional complications that may arise in the event of recession or lagging growth in the United States.

U.S. RESERVES AND BORROWING FACILITIES

The foregoing considerations suggest that the reserve needs of the United States cannot be judged by the same standards as might be relevant to the circumstances of other countries. At the end of November 1962 these reserves stood at $16,217 million, including $202 million of foreign convertible currencies, compared with a gold stock of close to $23 billion at the end of 1957. Over the same period United States liquid liabilities to foreign holders, both official and private, rose from $16.6 billion to $26.8 billion (end of September).[43] Some further reduction in reserves and increase in liabilities will doubtless occur before the gap in the balance of payments is closed. In particular, we need to be prepared for the possibility of further reserve losses if the United States succeeds in moving to a higher level of employment, even though, as noted at the end of Chapter III, a strengthening of the domestic economy could be expected to have positive as well as negative effects on the balance of payments.

This does not mean that reserves are now approaching a minimum beyond which the United States would be unable to finance further deficits.[44] How far the reduction might safely proceed is perhaps as much a matter of the rate of gold loss as of the absolute level of reserves. On the other hand, an appraisal of the reserve needs of the United States must also take account of the internal and external characteristics of the American economy summarized above, and allow for the eventuality of renewed disturbances and sluggish adjustments in the balance of payments.

[43] It will be clear from the preceding summation, however, that the reasons why the United States needs large reserves go well beyond those deriving from its position as an international reserve center, though this is the point most frequently stressed as distinguishing the United States, along with the United Kingdom, from other countries. Indeed, if it were not for these other reasons, any question about the adequacy of reserves would seem to reflect exaggerated concern. It may seem so in any event to British ears, since the United Kingdom operates on a much lower reserve ratio, with gold and convertible currency holdings of $2.8 billion (end of October 1962) and sterling liabilities of $9.7 billion (end of Sept. 1962). Three-fourths of the latter are, however, owed to countries of the sterling area, leaving $2,218 million owed to other countries. Moreover, the several sterling crises of recent years, the emergency fiscal and monetary measures which had to be taken at home, and the financial assistance extended by other countries to support sterling tend to confirm the view that "in any case, British reserves are much too small and cannot be the standard for determining the adequacy of U.S. reserves" (E. M. Bernstein, "The Adequacy of United States Gold Reserves," *American Economic Review*, Papers and Proceedings, May 1961, p. 441).

[44] One could perceive such a minimum, however, unless the requirement were waived that gold equal to at least 25 per cent of Federal Reserve notes in circulation and deposits be held against these liabilities. The amount of gold required for this purpose was $11.8 billion at the end of October 1962. Legislation to eliminate this requirement has been proposed but not passed. The Chairman of the Board of Governors of the Federal Reserve System has, however, given assurance that the Board would have full authority to suspend the requirement, should the reserve fall below the required minimum, and explained the mechanics of doing so (cf. Federal Reserve Bank of New York, *Monthly Review*, January 1963, p. 11).

The reserves held by the United States could be supplemented to some extent by the use of its drawing rights in the International Monetary Fund.[45] Without so far exercising these rights, the United States has, in fact, received $800 million in gold from the Fund during the last several years for the purchase by the Fund of income-earning U.S. Treasury bills and notes, of which $200 million was in 1956 (to provide the Fund with additional revenues for meeting administrative costs), $300 million in 1959, and a further $300 million in 1960.[46] The scope for a drawing by the United States has been limited, however, by the small amount of Fund assets useful and available for this purpose. Excluding dollars and also pounds sterling in view of the strained international financial position of the United Kingdom, the Fund's holdings of "major currencies"[47] at the end of October 1962 was $2.2 billion, of which half was in the currencies of Common Market countries and half in the currencies of Canada, Japan, and Sweden. In addition, the Fund then held $2.2 billion of gold, which could be sold to acquire any currencies that might be desired. On the other hand, the Fund's outstanding commitments under stand-by agreements with the United Kingdom and other countries amounted to $1.6 billion, and additional amounts would have to be held in reserve for possible drawings by other countries.

The resources available to the Fund might have been enlarged in various ways, including a further general increase in quotas; or a

---

[45] In his Message on Balance of Payments and Gold, February 6, 1961, the President indicated that the United States would exercise its drawing rights if and when appropriate. According to usual Fund practices, the United States would be able to purchase other currencies freely up to the amount of its "gold tranche" (i.e., one-quarter of its quota of $4,125 million) plus an amount equal to the outstanding amount of dollars purchased by other countries (though the amount of these purchases still outstanding on October 31, 1962, was only $36 million). A request for additional drawings up to a further 25 per cent of a country's quota would ordinarily be liberally treated, if it were making reasonable efforts to solve its balance-of-payments problems. Larger amounts would require "substantial justification" (cf. International Monetary Fund, *Annual Report 1962*, p. 31).

[46] The securities are held in the Fund's "gold account" and constitute a claim on U.S. gold stocks. These operations are additional to gold sales by the Fund to the United States of $600 million in 1957 and $150 million in 1961 to acquire dollars for use in meeting drawings by other members. See International Monetary Fund, *International Financial Statistics*, November 1962, pp. 4-8.

[47] That is, currencies of countries participating in the new agreement on "supplementary resources," described below.

selective increase in quotas which now appear unduly small, notably those of Western Germany ($787.5 million) and Italy ($270 million); or bilateral borrowings by the Fund from these countries or others in a strong balance-of-payments position. The method actually followed was the negotiation of a new multilateral agreement on "supplementary resources" among the United States and nine other leading industrial countries.[48] Under this agreement the participants have entered into stand-by commitments to lend their currencies to the Fund, up to specified amounts and subject to the agreement of the participants on each proposal, when needed "to forestall or cope with an impairment of the international monetary system." The amounts to be made available by countries other than the United States ($2 billion) and the United Kingdom ($1 billion) total $3 billion, of which $2,450 million would come from the Common Market countries and the remainder from Japan, Canada, and Sweden.[49]

The general purpose of the new agreement seems broad enough to cover any eventuality. Official comment, however, indicates that it is thought of primarily, if not solely, as one of the means[50] which have been developed for combating large speculative shifts of funds between different financial centers.[51] Whether, and on what conditions,

[48] The text of the agreement (called "Decision on General Arrangements to Borrow"), together with an accompanying letter from the French Minister of Finance to the Secretary of the United States Treasury, was published in a supplement to International Monetary Fund, *International Financial News Survey*, January 12, 1962.

[49] *The New York Times* of November 24, 1962, reported that Switzerland, subject to the approval of the Swiss Parliament, was prepared to participate in the ten-country arrangement to the equivalent of $200 million. Assistance by Switzerland (not a member of the IMF) would be extended by bilateral arrangement with the country in difficulty.

[50] See pp. 122-123 above for other elements in this defensive structure.

[51] In his address at the 1962 Annual Meeting of the International Monetary Fund, the Secretary of the Treasury spoke of the necessity of being able to cope with such movements and stated: "That is the significance of the special borrowing arrangements which are being established through the Fund by a number of the industrialized countries." Earlier, in testimony before the House Committee on Banking and Currency, the Secretary expressed the view that "the very existence of this large supplementary pool of usable resources should act as a strong deterrent to speculation against the dollar or other currencies" (Treasury press releases of February 27 and September 19, 1962). Also at the Fund meeting in 1962, the Chancellor of the Exchequer of the United Kingdom stated that "the resources made available under the borrowing scheme are not part of the normal stock of liquidity and it is deliberately designed to be used only in exceptional and extreme circumstances" (Press release No. 48, Boards of Governors 1962 Annual Meetings, September 19, 1962).

these additional resources could be called upon for assistance in financing deficits arising for other reasons is not clear. And even the resources available for countering speculative movements could be put to severe test, in time, if reserves and borrowing facilities for financing deficits on basic transactions were unduly depleted.

SOME ALTERNATIVE COURSES OF ACTION

The resources prospectively available to the United States, including its own reserves and its possibilities of borrowing from the International Monetary Fund, may not therefore fully correspond to the long-run needs of a country with the rather exceptional characteristics of the American economy.

In principle, additional resources to help tide over adjustment periods could be created by some form of mutual clearing and credit arrangement among countries whereby those in surplus would have their accounts credited, and those in deficit would have their accounts debited, in a common fund.[52] Such facilities would be provided, for instance, by Triffin's plan for centralizing monetary reserves in an expanded International Monetary Fund, with powers to lend and invest. His proposals appear, however, to be mainly directed toward reducing the risk of disruptive withdrawals of official balances from countries now serving as reserve centers and toward providing for the future growth of international liquidity in ways less subject to this risk.[53] Balance-of-payments problems were doubtless uppermost in the mind of the Chancellor of the Exchequer of the United Kingdom when, in his address at the 1962 meeting of the International Monetary Fund, he suggested that study be given to "a system of cooperation between the leading trading countries in the form of a mutual currency account in the Fund." He further described this as "an arrangement of a multilateral character under which countries could continue to acquire the currency of another country which was temporarily surplus in the markets and use it to establish claims on a mutual currency account which

---

[52] For an analysis of various proposals that would correspond to this general formulation, see Fritz Machlup, *Plans for Reform of the International Monetary System*, Princeton University, Special Papers in International Economics, No. 3, August 1962.

[53] Triffin, *Gold and the Dollar Crisis.*

they could themselves use when their situations were reversed."[54]

However great their logical force and their potentialities for strengthening the international monetary system, proposals for action along these lines encounter a familiar and stubborn difficulty. That is the problem of reaching agreement among countries on (1) the amounts of financing which individual members may be asked to provide or may be entitled to receive, and (2) the degree of automaticity or conditionality attaching to these obligations and rights.[55] These are questions on which countries with balance-of-payments surpluses are likely to take more restrictive views than those with deficits. And the first are inevitably in a stronger bargaining position than the second.

[54] Press release of September 19, 1962, cited above. The Chancellor also expressed the hope "that such a system would enable world liquidity to be expanded without additional strains on the reserve currencies or avoidable setbacks to their economic growth, and at the same time without requiring countries whose currencies were temporarily strong to accumulate larger holdings of weaker currencies than they would find tolerable."

[55] Triffin's views do not appear to be very fully set forth on these questions. Under his plan the growth in world liquidity would come through (1) investments in securities of member countries undertaken at the initiative of the Fund and (2) advances granted by the Fund in response to members' needs for borrowing. The distribution of the Fund's investments by countries could present difficulties, as Triffin recognizes in the various alternatives which he has suggested (investment in the less developed countries, investment in bonds of the International Bank for relending to the less developed countries, or investment in the established money markets of the developed countries). But perhaps the thorniest problem revolves around the principles and rules which would govern access to the Fund's resources by countries in balance-of-payments difficulty. At one point Triffin states that the Fund's lending operations "should be no more automatic than they are at present, and this discretion should enable it to exercise a considerable influence upon members to restrain internal inflationary abuses." Along the same line, he indicates that under his plan the "discipline of gold outflows" would be strengthened and (without specifying what corrective measures would have been appropriate) that the United States would not have been able to run such large deficits as in recent years. (Cf. Harris, ed., *The Dollar in Crisis*, pp. 236, 285.) In testimony before the Joint Economic Committee, on the other hand, Triffin has suggested that the expanded Fund, by investing in the United States on its own initiative rather than lending in response to the initiative of the United States, would be able to come quietly to this country's assistance and help "to buy the time necessary for effecting, in as smooth a manner as possible—in the interest of other countries as well as in our own—the readjustment of our current overall balance-of-payments deficits" (reprinted in *Gold and the Dollar Crisis*, p. 13). These passages are alike in depicting a Fund of great power, but convey rather different impressions of how that power would be exercised. They are indicative of the problems that would arise in renegotiating the Fund's Articles of Agreement.

These differences were apparent in the Keynes and White plans elaborated during the last war, and in the decisions taken at the Bretton Woods Conference in 1944 and embodied in the Articles of Agreement of the International Monetary Fund. They seem to be apparent also in the discussion and terms of the new agreement on supplementary resources.[56]

Today, the distinctive features of this country's position suggest that it may need access to larger and more assured means of financing as a safeguard against future contingencies. Yet it is difficult to see how any general formula could be developed that would be adequate to the peculiarities and responsibilities of its own position without imposing greater lending commitments on other countries than they would wish to assume or conferring greater borrowing facilities than most of them might legitimately require. The difficulty of composing differences in views on these questions seems to underlie the lack of enthusiasm by United States monetary authorities with regard to "heroic new proposals for international liquidity."[57]

Unless satisfactory compromises can be worked out on these issues, the United States may need to persevere in the adjustments which it is making to the point of achieving not merely a balance but a surplus

[56] See the letter mentioned in note 48 from the French Minister of Finance setting forth the procedures to be followed in drawing on the supplementary resources, including the stipulation that, if the participants are not in unanimous agreement, the prospective borrower will not be entitled to vote. The Bank for International Settlements in its Annual Report for the year ended March 31, 1962, comments (p. 18): "The special procedure agreed upon . . . provides safeguards by leaving the principal decisions in the hands of the lending countries." A private source interprets the provisions of the agreement as meaning that "in practice the task of watching over the monetary discipline of a given country will be entrusted to its potential creditors—a task that was performed automatically by the classic gold standard." (Union Bank of Switzerland, *Bulletin,* October 1961.)

[57] See testimony by Under Secretary Roosa on December 13, 1962, before the Subcommittee on International Exchange and Payments of the Joint Economic Committee. Roosa explained his position as follows:

". . . . Unless surplus countries are willing and able to extend credit, on terms and through media which are acceptable to deficit countries, there will not in fact be additional international credit, whatever the formal arrangements may seem to be. . . . It is relatively easy to draw up a plan for a systematic monetary network of conduits, pools, and valves for the storage and release of international credit. It is a very different task to induce creditors and debtors to put into that network the credit itself—without which the whole mechanism remains on the drawing-board, or if it exists, has little practical significance.

"For in the world of today, I feel reasonably sure, no country will undertake in advance an automatic liability for the extension of large amounts of credit. . . ."

in its international payments so as to strengthen its own reserves once again. When, and with what vigor, this objective could be pursued would have to be determined in relation to other considerations, including the state of the domestic economy. The United States, is, however, subject to yet another inhibition as long as it serves as the world's leading reserve center and source of liquidity. The logic of its present role in the international monetary system may tend to keep it more often in deficit than in surplus as world demand for reserves rises gradually with the growth of trade or as some countries seek to bolster their present positions. The United Kingdom, with its own responsibilities as a reserve center, and perhaps Japan are the only major trading and financial countries whose reserves seem to be still in need of strengthening. Those of most other Western European countries look adequate or more than adequate. They may not all take the same view of the matter, however, and this may be more relevant to their policies than any rule-of-thumb calculation of the appropriate level of reserves. Under these conditions, policy conflicts with risks of deflationary consequences could arise if the United States and several other leading countries were all seeking to increase, and none willing to lose, reserves.

If it is not looking too far and too hopefully into the future, the inhibition against a balance-of-payments surplus by the United States could be removed or reduced if the United States were to accumulate official reserves in other strong currencies, so that its surplus would not require reductions in other countries' gold and dollar reserves.[58] The United States has, in fact, already taken some steps in this direction and apparently contemplates the possibility of moving further toward accumulating "some moderate amounts of the convertible exchange of various leading countries."[59] To provide resources adequate to assure

[58] Cf. Xenophon Zolotas, *Towards a Reinforced Gold Exchange Standard*, Athens, 1961.

[59] See address by Under Secretary Roosa, at the Monetary Conference of the American Bankers Association, Rome, Italy, May 17, 1962 (Treasury press release).

The action of the Federal Open Market Committee authorizing Federal Reserve operations in foreign currencies (see page 122 above) included among the "specific aims" of these transactions: "In the long run, to provide a means whereby reciprocal holdings of foreign currencies may contribute to meeting needs for international liquidity as required in terms of an expanding world economy" (from text of authorization as quoted in Federal Reserve Bank of New York, *Monthly Review*, October 1962).

its own position without weakening that of others, the store of convertible exchange which needs to be built up could run into substantial amounts. How much is needed would depend on several things. One would be the amount of any further losses in our monetary reserves or increases in our liquid liabilities. Another would be the size and nature of any new mutual credit facilities and other arrangements that may be agreed upon with other countries. Still more important would be the degree to which we succeed in making the American economy more flexible and adaptable in response to the requirements of its external position. Two problems already stressed in this study appear to be of paramount importance in this regard: (1) the adjustment of wages and prices in the light of productivity gains and international competitive conditions, and (2) the harmonization of monetary, fiscal, and other instruments of general economic policy to meet our domestic objectives without releasing excessive outflows of capital. More broadly considered, unless satisfactory solutions can be found to these problems, even very large reserves would not ensure the survival of a regime of exchange rate stability.

At the conclusion of this report it is appropriate to stress, as already noted in the Preface, the exploratory character of the analysis. It has been directed chiefly toward identifying problems, especially those on which further research is needed, though at the same time the study seeks to illuminate these problems as far as the present state of knowledge and the summary nature of this essay permit. Policies have been discussed, not with a view to arriving at specific proposals, but rather in order to indicate possible choices and some of the principle considerations which need to be kept in mind in weighing them.

APPENDIX A

A Note on Alternative Ways
of Presenting the Balance of Payments

It has seemed useful in this study to stress the new importance of international movements of liquid capital for the balance of payments and for economic policy, and, without losing sight of certain interrelations, to distinguish these movements from other international transactions. The present note extends the discussion and considers the implications of the increased international mobility of liquid capital for the definition and presentation of the balance of payments.

It is hoped that this discussion, though brief and exploratory, will provide some new perspectives on issues which have long engaged the attention of international trade theorists and balance-of-payments specialists and contribute to the development of thought about some of our current problems.

Direct repetition of ideas dealt with in the main body of this paper has been held to a minimum, and this note should be read in conjunction with the relevant portions of Chapters II and IV, especially pages 11-17 and 117-126.

1. *The Search for an Organizing Concept*

For the United States or any other country committed to exchange rate stability, with unrestricted convertibility into other currencies, a central point in any concept of the balance of payments concerns the country's ability to assure an adequate command over internationally acceptable means of payment with which to defend the external value of its currency. The balance of payments, as a statistical digest of a country's international transactions,[1] is looked to in this context as a basis for explaining the past and as a guide to the future. Many factors must, of course, be considered in addition to those directly observable in the balance-of-payments accounts. These include the general state of demand and employment at home and abroad, changes in the relative levels of costs and prices, shifts in demand and supply affecting particular products, and conditions influencing the international flow of capital. No method of organizing and presenting the balance of payments can be self-explanatory. Some may, however, provide a better starting point for analysis and policy formation than others. Or, if no one method clearly commends itself above the rest, a consideration of alternative methods may at least reveal their various shortcomings.

If all transactions are accounted for, the balance of payments must balance—that is, it will add algebraically to zero. The identification of a "surplus" or "deficit" therefore involves the segregation of certain items from the main body of the balance of payments as being different in some significant respect from the rest. The question of presenting and measuring the balance of payments can thus be posed in terms of the search for a suitable distinguishing principle or organizing concept for determining which items are to be placed in the main body of the balance of payments ("above the line") and which are to be placed outside ("below the line"). Account being taken of errors and omissions ("unrecorded transactions"), both groups of items will net out to the same figure with opposite signs.

The view developed here is that the nation's international transactions can usefully be grouped according to the main causal forces operating on them and, hence, according to the types of policy action affecting them. This approach, as applied in the present study, leads to the division of the accounts into two groups on the basis of the degree of sensitivity to monetary conditions and policies. The balance computed in this way corresponds to that sometimes called the "basic

---

[1] It may be noted that the expression "balance of payments" is commonly used to refer to either, or even simultaneously to both, of two ideas: (1) the statistical summary of a country's international receipts and payments over a given period or (2) the surplus or deficit shown by such a statement, computed as the difference between certain of its items.

balance," though the expression "balance on basic transactions" would seem more appropriate and will be employed in this paper.[2] The method of grouping the accounts employed since the war by the Department of Commerce is based on a different objective, described as that of measuring changes in the nation's "international liquidity."[3]

Summary statements corresponding to the two principal alternatives discussed here are given in Table A-1.[4] It will be seen that the difference between the two arrangements derives from the disposition of two items—recorded movements of United States private short-term capital and unrecorded transactions—changes in which are believed to reflect largely also movements of liquid funds.[5] The question is

[2] In an area in which terminological confusion thrives, the expression "basic balance" or "basic deficit" seems particularly unsuitable and misleading since it may appear to mean that special adjustments have been made to arrive at some measure of the basic disequilibrium or "hard-core" deficit (for instance, allowances for increased imports at higher levels of employment, for abnormal elements in exports, such as a lumping of jet aircraft deliveries during a short period of time, etc).

On the other hand, the expression "over-all balance," frequently used to designate the Commerce Department's definition, also suffers from lack of precision and may be misleading. As will be clear from an examination of Table 1 (Chapter II), it is less comprehensive in the types of transactions placed "above the line" than the "official settlements" version of the balance, which, as noted below, some would prefer.

[3] Recently, the Commerce Department has introduced in its reports, on an experimental basis, a supplementary presentation with a division corresponding to the balance on basic transactions and containing certain useful details as well, especially with regard to the Government's own international operations. (See Table 2 in the articles on the balance of payments in the *Survey of Current Business* for March, June, and September 1962.) This new presentation employs the term "Balance on Goods and Services, Government Assistance, and Long-Term Capital Accounts" for what is here more briefly called "Balance on Basic Transactions."

[4] The left side of the table is condensed from the familiar summary Table 1 appearing regularly in the quarterly balance-of-payments articles in the *Survey of Current Business*, and all references in the present note to the tabular representation of the Commerce Department's concepts are to that source.

[5] As discussed in Chapter II, the entry for unrecorded transactions presents serious analytical difficulties, registering as it does the net effect of all errors and omissions in the balance-of-payments estimates. There seems to be little doubt, however, that the big changes observable in the item have been closely associated with short-term capital movements. This also seems to be the conclusion pointed to in the *Survey of Current Business*, September 1960, which introduced a review of the significance of fluctuations in the residual during the postwar period with the following observation: "The close relationship between the changes in the net of unrecorded transactions in the balance of payments and conditions which can be expected to induce such short-term capital movements is indicated by the experiences during the postwar period."

TABLE A-1

SUMMARY SCHEMATA FOR ALTERNATIVE WAYS OF
PRESENTING THE BALANCE OF PAYMENTS
(billions of dollars)

	I. Based on Concept of "Net International Liquidity"	1958-1959 (average)	1960-1961 (average)
	ITEMS TREATED AS MAKING UP the "OVER-ALL BALANCE"		
1.	*U.S. payments, recorded*	28.6	31.6
2.	Imports of goods and services	22.1	23.1
3.	Remittances and pensions	.8	.9
4.	U.S. government grants and credits	3.1	3.7
5.	U.S. private long-term capital	2.5	2.5
6.	U.S. private short-term capital	.2	1.4
7.	*U.S. receipts, recorded*	24.5	29.0
8.	Exports of goods and services	23.3	27.6
9.	Repayments on U.S. government loans	.8	1.0
10.	Foreign capital, excluding liquid funds	.4	.4
11.	*Unrecorded transactions net*	.4	— .6
12.	*Balance on items listed above*	—3.6	—3.2
	ITEMS TREATED AS MEASURING CHANGE IN "NET INTERNATIONAL LIQUIDITY"		
13.	Gold and convertible currency holdings of U.S. monetary authorities	1.5	1.2
14.	Liquid liabilities to foreign and international monetary authorities	1.2	1.2
15.	Liquid liabilities to foreign commercial banks and other private or international holders	1.0	.8

(continued)

140

TABLE A-1 (concluded)

	II. Based on Concept of "Sensitivity to Monetary Policy"	1958-1959 (average)	1960-1961 (average)
	ITEMS TREATED AS MAKING UP THE "BALANCE ON BASIC TRANSACTIONS"		
1.	U.S. payments, recorded	28.4	30.2
2.	Imports of goods and services	22.1	23.1
3.	Remittances and pensions	.8	.9
4.	U.S. government grants and credits	3.1	3.7
5.	U.S. private long-term capital	2.5	2.5
6.	U.S. receipts, recorded	24.5	28.9
7.	Exports of goods and services	23.3	27.6
8.	Repayments on U.S. government loans	.8	1.0
9.	Foreign long-term investment in U.S.	.4	.4
10.	Balance on items listed above	—3.9	—1.2
	ITEMS TREATED AS "SENSITIVE TO MONETARY POLICY"		
11.	Gold and convertible currency holdings of U.S. monetary authorities	1.5	1.2
12.	Liquid liabilities to foreign and international monetary authorities	1.2	1.2
13.	Liquid liabilities to foreign and commercial banks and other private or international holders	1.0	.8
14.	U.S. private short-term capital[a]	— .1	—1.4
15.	Unrecorded transactions, net	.4	— .6

[a] Less changes in foreign commercial credits to the United States.

SOURCE: Table B-1.

NOTE: Detail may not add to totals shown because of rounding.

141

whether these items should be placed "above the line," as is the current practice of the Commerce Department (left half of table), or "below the line," as the alternative approach suggested here (right half of table) would have it. Similar questions may be raised with regard to some of the other capital items, as will be seen later.

It is apparent that the way this question is decided has an important bearing on the measurement of the deficit. When the net flow of funds in the form of reported U.S. short-term capital or through unrecorded transactions is outward, as in 1960 and 1961, the adverse balance as computed by the Commerce Department will be greater than that indicated by the alternative method. The opposite result is produced when these flows are inward, as was true, on balance, of the 1950's.

It is no mere coincidence that interest in alternative approaches to the balance of payments has greatly increased in recent years with the appearance of large deficits in this country's international accounts. The subject itself is, however, much older. Both of the principal concepts considered in this paper have their antecedents in the history of balance-of-payments theory, and enough will be said of still other approaches to indicate the considerable diversity of thought and practice in this area. One should therefore not assume that there has hitherto been some unique way of measuring the deficit or surplus which is only now being called into question.

2. *The Concept of International Liquidity*

The liquidity concept underlying the Commerce Department's familiar summary balance-of-payments tables has been explained by Walther Lederer, the officer in charge of this area of the Department's work. After stating that the purpose is "to measure the changes in our capability to defend the exchange value of the dollar," he adds: "This defense is the responsibility of our monetary authorities and their capability depends upon their liquid resources and the liquid claims which can be exercised against these resources."[6]

[6] "Measuring the Balance of Payments," in American Statistical Association, *1961 Proceedings of the Business and Economics Statistics Section,* Washington, 1962, p. 45. See also Lederer's contribution, "The Balance of United States Payments: A Statement of the Problem," in Seymour E. Harris (ed.), *The Dollar in Crisis,* New York, 1961, pp. 114-136. These articles, though written in a personal capacity, are a fuller exposition of the concepts expressed in the regular balance-of-payments articles carried in the *Survey of Current Business* (see, for example, the issues for September 1960, p. 10, and March 1962, pp. 19-21).

The liquid resources referred to in Lederer's statement include the country's gold reserves and, since March 1961, convertible foreign currencies held by our monetary authorities (i.e., Treasury and Federal Reserve). The liquid liabilities include all foreign-owned bank balances and other short-term assets in the United States together with U.S. Government securities (of all maturities) held by foreigners, whether official or private, and including also international agencies, both monetary and other. Decreases in our liquid resources or increases in our liquid liabilities reduce our international liquidity, and changes of the opposite nature increase it. The sum of the changes in these various items is thus taken to measure the net change in our international liquidity and hence the "surplus" or "deficit" corresponding to this concept.

ALTERNATIVE WAYS OF TREATING U.S. LIABILITIES

Questions may be raised as to whether certain of these items should be treated differently in the measurement of the deficit. There is considerable support for a definition whereby only official settlements between the monetary authorities would be entered "below the line," and changes in liabilities to commercial banks and other foreign holders would be entered "above the line."[7] Though all foreign assets here can be regarded as potential claims on our reserves, the case for making a distinction according to the official or unofficial status of the holder appears rather strong. Private claims on the United States, by commercial banks and others, are sometimes discussed as if they were merely the passive result, or even reluctant acceptance, of the backwash of our own balance-of-payments deficits. There may be such an element in balances held here on official account, especially to the extent that

---

[7] Table 1, Chapter II, shows the composition of the deficit on the official settlements basis compared with other definitions, and the discussion on pp. 18-19 points to some of the practical problems arising in the application of this concept. See also Gardner's and Triffin's views discussed later in this note.

foreign central banks or governments, to support the dollar, may refrain from converting as much of their dollar accruals into gold as they would otherwise do. But the large accumulation of short-term assets here by foreign commercial banks and other holders, excluding monetary authorities—rising from $3.1 billion at the end of 1949 to $5.7 billion at the end of 1957 and to $8.2 billion at the end of September 1962—is to be explained, in the main, as the deliberate acquisition of dollar funds for the useful purposes which they serve.

It may also be noted that the presentation of the United States balance of payments in the recent Annual Reports of the International Monetary Fund[8] corresponds to yet another definition of the deficit, whereby the items entered "below the line" include changes in short-term and other liquid liabilities to official institutions and also to commercial banks, but not to other private holders.

The foregoing questions relate to the inclusion or exclusion of certain foreign claims according to the status of the holder as reported in the statistics. Still other questions arise as to whether certain components of these assets, if they could be separately identified by the reporting system, should be segregated from foreign liquid claims on the United States. For instance, the compensating balances which foreign borrowers are required to keep on deposit, generally ranging from 15 to 20 per cent of the amount borrowed, are not really liquid. Similarly, banks in other countries accepting dollar deposits (creating so-called "Euro-dollar" accounts) find it necessary to immobilize a substantial part of the dollar assets so acquired against their dollar liabilities. In practice, it might well be impossible to distinguish these from other foreign assets. The Commerce Department has, however, begun to segregate (and enter above the line) changes in foreign commercial credits to the United States.

ASYMMETRY IN TREATMENT OF ASSETS AND LIABILITIES

The most distinctive and debatable feature of the Commerce Department's practice is the difference in treatment accorded American private short-term capital compared with that given to foreign private short-term capital, movements in the former being entered above the line and movements in the latter below. This practice has been criti-

---

[8] See p. 80 (1960) and p. 81 (1961).

cized, by myself among others, as asymmetrical.[9] Thus, if an American bank and a foreign bank exchanged deposits, each crediting the other with $100, the two operations would not cancel out in the Commerce Department's presentation. Instead, the rise in American short-term assets abroad would appear above the line with a minus sign as an outflow of capital contributing to the deficit, and the rise in foreign short-term assets here would appear below the line with a plus sign as a direct measure (with signs reversed) of the deficit.

The point has also been made that the Commerce Department's practice, if universalized, would lead to mutually inconsistent results in that, in a time of generally rising international financial transactions, several financial centers might simultaneously record an increase in foreign private claims on them without reporting any offsetting assets. To revert to the illustration in the preceding paragraph (and barring other transactions), both the United States and the foreign country concerned would show a balance-of-payments deficit of 100 on this basis. The risk is that a number of leading countries might become simultaneously concerned about a deterioration or lack of improvement in their individual balances of payments and engage in mutually conflicting policies in the effort to strengthen them. That this risk is not altogether negligible is suggested by a recent analysis of differences in national statistical practices appearing in the *Staff Papers* of the International Monetary Fund.[10]

In reply to these criticisms, Lederer has stressed that, unlike foreign private short-term claims on the United States, United States private short-term assets abroad are only in part in the form of liquid claims on other leading financial centers and include large amounts of trade and other credits to countries, especially Japan and some of the Latin American countries, which could not be quickly mobilized in

[9] In a paper presented at the American Economic Association in December 1960, "Disturbances and Adjustments in Recent U.S. Balance-of-Payments Experience." *American Economic Review*, May 1961, pp. 417-429.

More detailed criticisms were formulated by Walter R. Gardner ("An Exchange-Market Analysis of the U.S. Balance of Payments," *IMF Staff Papers*, May 1961, pp. 195-211). Further reference to his criticisms and proposals is made later in this appendix.

[10] Poul Høst-Madsen, "Asymmetries Between Balance of Payments Surpluses and Deficits," *IMF Staff Papers*, July 1962, pp. 182-198. See also the article "What, No Creditors?" *The Economist*, January 20, 1962, p. 254.

case of need.[11] He has drawn the further important distinction that American private short-term assets abroad are less surely available to our monetary authorities, if needed, than would be true in the reverse case of foreign private liquid claims on us. The reason for this distinction lies in the difference in the degree of influence or control exercised over the national money market and banking operations by American monetary authorities compared with their foreign counterparts.[12]

Shortcomings in the Liquidity Concept

If the relevant test is the certainty and speed with which funds, once invested internationally, can be *repatriated*, it is hard to find serious fault in the Commerce Department's practice. On the Department's definition, however, the liquidity criterion itself may suffer from certain deficiencies in relation to the broad objective assigned to it—that is, to measure changes in the ability of the United States to defend the exchange value of the dollar. It would seem that the Commerce Department's approach to this objective is sharply focused on the eventuality of a currency crisis in which all *foreign* liquid claims on this country are suddenly exercised. The question implicit in that approach is: How has the capability of the United States to meet such a crisis altered, during any given balance-of-payments accounting period, as the result of changes in our gold or other official reserves and in foreign official and private claims on them?

First of all, one may ask if this question is not rather narrowly formulated as a regular guide to the state of the balance of payments. Our liquid assets and liabilities sometimes change for reasons which have little to do with the fundamental factors in our international payments position. It will be suggested in a moment that, within the limits of what can be gleaned from this or that way of looking at the data, the balance on basic transactions is probably a better guide to this country's ability to defend the dollar than the net change in international liquidity.

The eventuality of a convertibility crisis is, however, also a legitimate and necessary concern. But in this regard the Commerce Department's concept of international liquidity is subject to the further criti-

---

[11] See Table 5, Chapter II.

[12] For a fuller statement of Lederer's views on these points, see the references mentioned in footnote 6.

cism that changes in foreign liquid claims on us relate to only a part of the potential demands on our reserves. It is a measurable part and also a strategic part, since foreign-owned balances are doubtless particularly sensitive to changing conditions at home and abroad. But this last observation is also true, and perhaps increasingly so, of large though not readily identifiable parts of American-owned dollar funds. *All* liquid assets in this country—not merely the smaller part of the whole which is owned abroad—may be regarded as potential claims on United States reserves in that they may be exchanged for other currencies and thereby accrue to foreign central banks entitled to request conversion into gold.[13] Events of the last three years have demonstrated that the monetary authorities must be prepared to reckon with, and may have to counteract or curb, large outflows of American private funds and also those outflows which appear to be hidden in the errors and omissions item.[14]

It is true that there is no way whereby the balance of payments could take account of changes in financial conditions or psychological attitudes that may add to, or subtract from, potential *domestic* demands on our gold reserves through capital transfers abroad. But this difficulty serves to emphasize the limitations inherent in the international liquidity concept as a guide to the balance of payments. It might seem that one should at least include in our payments to other countries (i.e., "above the line") the amount of American private short-term capital which has actually moved abroad in any given period as giving some kind of indication of what the future outflow of this nature could amount to. The burden of the argument developed here is that the one does not provide even the roughest kind of guide to the other, and that an assessment of potential future capital outflows must reckon with many

[13] The frequently invoked analogy with a bank (though perhaps useful for devising titles to papers such as this one) will thus be seen as an oversimplification, and points to a limitation in the concept of net international liquidity as a basis for measuring the balance of payments or for assessing changes in the capability of the authorities to defend the dollar. A bank cannot be confronted with a drain from within on its liquid resources (unless the officers make off with the cash), but a nation can be faced with this problem and sometimes is.

[14] This point has been strongly emphasized by Walter Gardner: "In short, there is virtually no limit to the amount of U.S. funds that could flow abroad if the inducements were sufficient. The picture that the Department of Commerce balancing item gives of the changes in the ratio of reserves to certain liabilities is a picture that touches only the fringe of this potential problem. The greatest possibilities for mischief lie in the very categories that are omitted from the Commerce package" (*IMF Staff Papers*, May 1961, pp. 203-204).

factors, including above all the ability of the monetary authorities to pursue policies aimed at keeping such flows within tolerable limits.

3. *An Alternative Concept*: *Sensitivity to Monetary Policy*

It is the particular concern of the monetary authorities with international movements of liquid funds that provides the clue to the organizing concept employed in the present study. This approach attempts to distinguish between our international transactions according to their sensitivity to monetary policy, those judged to be relatively sensitive being placed below the line and the rest above.

Monetary policy is here thought of as policy affecting the terms on which capital can be lent and borrowed, including not only the. activities of the Federal Reserve banks but also the debt management operations of the Treasury. It would also include any taxes, special charges, or other discrimination, other than that which the market itself may establish, between the terms available to domestic borrowers and lenders and those available to foreign borrowers and lenders—a point of greater relevance at present to foreign monetary regimes than to that of the United States. For present purposes, moreover, monetary policy should include any intervention by the authorities in the foreign exchange market such as to influence spot or forward rates.

The concept of sensitivity to monetary policy, as applied to international transactions, includes the notions of certainty of response, speed of response, and magnitude of response, the idea being that certain transactions are likely to be generally more responsive than others in all three respects or in some weighted combination of them. Further research, and perhaps further experience under recently restored conditions of currency convertibility, will be needed to test the validity of this distinction and, if valid, to determine how individual types of transactions should be classified.

THE STRATEGIC ROLE OF THE BASIC TRANSACTIONS

The transactions to be placed above the line according to the sensitivity concept would be those which are influenced chiefly by general economic forces, as in the case of foreign trade and investments, or by our political and military objectives, as in the case of government expenditures for military purposes and foreign aid.

As noted in Chapter II, responsibility for policies affecting these various types of transactions is dispersed, except as these policies are coordinated at the highest levels of government. Monetary policy has little or no effect on some of these items and influences others only indirectly and gradually through changes in incomes, prices, and profit expectations.

Variations in these transactions may be great, both relatively and absolutely, and have major effects on the balance of payments. They do not necessarily move, however, in the direction needed for balance-of-payments adjustments and may not be readily amenable to policy changes determined by these purposes. Seen in a balance-of-payments context, these transactions tend to be slow to adjust and are sometimes perverse in their behavior.

It is, however, also appropriate to describe them as "basic transactions," since their combined behavior provides a measure of the adequacy of this country's competitive strength and its "capability to defend the exchange value of the dollar." Changes in the balance on basic transactions are therefore bound to be of distinct and strategic interest in an evaluation of our balance-of-payments strength or weakness and in the determination of policies affecting these items.

THE TACTICAL ROLE OF THE SENSITIVE ITEMS

The items to be grouped below the line would be those which are relatively sensitive to monetary policy and which are therefore the particular responsibility of the monetary authorities. They include, first of all, changes in official holdings of gold and convertible currencies for the reason that these assets can always be sold to support the currency. They also include those movements of private liquid funds, both foreign and American, which are influenced by differences in monetary conditions at home and abroad.

By their nature, these sensitive items can be made to serve only in a temporary or tactical capacity to alleviate, or to avoid adding to, strains arising elsewhere in the balance of payments. They could not indefinitely compensate a serious imbalance in basic transactions. Indeed, if confidence in the strength of the currency weakens under such conditions, the flow of liquid capital may react adversely and add to the loss of reserves. Even in the absence of such conditions, flows of liquid funds are not to be thought of merely as passive "balancing items." This would tend to be true of official funds (except when central banks or governments are, for example, borrowing for the specific purpose of building up their reserves). But movements of private funds are motivated by many factors, ranging all the way from meeting the needs of foreign customers and acquiring working balances to transfers of idle funds in search of higher yields.

It must be noted, moreover, that private short-term capital transactions may themselves exert a causal influence on the balance of basic transactions. This is notably true with regard to the provision of export credits, which may be as important as price or other factors in our competitive position in foreign markets. Exports and export financing by the United States are thus not independent of each other—as they would tend to be if the facilities of the various national money markets were open to all countries without being tied to exports or otherwise restricted. A reduction in the net flow of export credit from the United States would therefore tend to mean some reduction also in United States exports. The effect may be a good deal less than one-for-one, however, since credits extended by American banks serve to finance imports not only from the United States but also from third countries, or to release other funds for this purpose, and since foreign borrowers do, in fact, have considerable and increasing access to other sources of financing, as discussed below.

The key question concerns the ability of the American monetary authorities to act so as to obtain—when needed—a net benefit to our reserve position, whether by *inducing an inflow* of funds or by *curtailing an outflow*.[15] This two-pronged statement of the question, it should be noted, contrasts with the focus of the liquidity concept on the difficulty and uncertainty of effecting a quick repatriation of American private short-term assets abroad. The chief problem may be

[15] Much the same view was expressed in the *Survey of Current Business,* December 1960, p. 10, which summed up its analysis as follows: "The recent balance of payments developments suggest, therefore, two problems: The immediate requirement of checking the outflow of short-term capital, and the longer range requirement of bringing about a further improvement in the balance on our major interchange." It may also be noted that this statement seems to make about the same distinction as that suggested in the present paper between basic transactions and items sensitive to monetary policy. The statement would seem to be still valid as a characterization of our balance-of-payments position on the basis of developments through the first nine months of 1962, marked by the renewal of large-scale outflows of liquid funds in the third quarter (as far as can be judged by the behavior of "unrecorded transactions").

simply to prevent, or reduce, the further outflow of funds into such assets, irrespective of whether, or how quickly, the assets outstanding can be enticed home again. The same contribution, in absolute amount, to the strengthening of the balance of payments is made when an outflow of, say, 1,000 is reduced to one of 500 as when an outflow of 300 is replaced by an inflow of 200. The practical significance of this point and of the distinction made with the liquidity concept stands out clearly enough in relation to the size of the recorded and unrecorded outflows in 1960 and 1961.

Even so, it should not be supposed that American private short-term assets abroad are completely illiquid. This would scarcely be true of unreported American short-term funds abroad—an element which may be overlooked in evaluations of liquidity based on what is known about the composition of reported assets. With respect to the latter, moreover, it seems reasonable to assign a fairly high degree of liquidity to claims on leading foreign financial centers, amounting to some $2 billion at the end of 1961, or about one-third of the total short-term claims on all foreign countries as reported by American banks and nonfinancial concerns. For the rest, it is doubtless true that most other countries would not be able, in the typical case, to reduce their *total* foreign short-term indebtedness very quickly, or perhaps not at all. But, as their obligations to American lenders mature, they may be induced by appropriate changes in our policies to undertake some refinancing in foreign money markets, including the active and well-supplied Euro-dollar market.[16] The significance and future potentialities of this relatively new source of financing should not be overlooked, since foreign commercial banks have large holdings of dollars and ready access to more through the Euro-dollar market and their own central banks.[17] Such credit operations in dollar funds between for-

[16] There is sometimes a tendency, it seems, to confuse (1) the liquidity, or lack of it, of *total* foreign claims on a particular country and (2) the liquidity of a *particular claim or set of claims* on that country. Even a country which is over-extended in its total external short-term indebtedness may find it advantageous, if interest differentials change, to shift, for instance, some of its acceptance financing from New York to other centers.

[17] A comprehensive description of the Euro-dollar market has been provided by Oscar L. Altman in two papers, "Foreign Markets for Dollars, Sterling and Other Currencies" *IMF Staff Papers*, December 1961, pp. 313-352, and "Recent Developments in Foreign Markets for Dollars and Other Currencies," in *Factors Affecting the United States Balance of Payments* (Joint Economic Committee), Washington, December 1962, pp. 483-523.

eigners, it must be remembered, do not add to the total amount of foreign liquid claims on the United States but rather, as previously noted, tend to make these claims less liquid than they would otherwise be. Moreover, operations in the international Euro-dollar market, though competing with the national money markets of other countries, are largely free from the restrictions applied in some of these markets.

4. *The Question of What to Include Among the Sensitive Items*

Stress is frequently placed on the practical difficulty of making a meaningful distinction between "short-term" and "long-term" capital movements—the fact that these terms do not necessarily mean what they may appear to; that statistics can only be based on the maturities of the assets acquired, those maturing in one year or less being considered, in United States practice, short-term and others long-term; that these maturities may not correspond to the intentions of the owners of the assets; and that their intentions may in any event change, so that funds placed in long maturities may be withdrawn after only a short time or, contrariwise, funds placed in short maturities may be continuously reinvested in similar or other assets, or may not be available upon maturity because of the inability of the borrower, or borrowing country, to make payment. The statistical data available may therefore match rather poorly with theoretical concepts or analytical needs.[18]

This difficulty is less serious than might at first appear when we seek to apply the sensitivity criterion. It will have become clear from the preceding discussion that, under this concept, references to the "outflow of private liquid funds" concern their liquidity and sensitivity to monetary conditions *at the time the flow takes place* and not simply their liquidity, or lack of it, *after* the flow has occurred. Under present conditions, it may be less important for the United States to be able to reverse the direction of the net movement than to influence, as may be needed, the size of the outflows. We are therefore more concerned with

---

[18] Discussions of these problems will be found in "Inflows and Outflows of Foreign Funds," Bank of England, *Quarterly Bulletin,* June 1962, pp. 93 ff., and "Short-term Capital Movements and the United States Balance of Payments," Federal Reserve Bank of New York, *Monthly Review,* July 1962, pp. 94 ff.

the behavioral characteristics of the outflows in this regard than with the length of life of the assets acquired.

RESPONSIVENESS OF SHORT-TERM CAPITAL TO MONETARY POLICY

The susceptibility of short-term capital flows to the influence of monetary policy should be subject to empirical test, though, in fact, the conditions necessary for such a test have existed for only a relatively short time in postwar experience. Thus the balance-of-payments article in the December 1960 issue of the *Survey of Current Business* commented as follows:

International investments of liquid capital, particularly purchases and sales of negotiable short-term obligations such as acceptances and Treasury bills, and changes in deposits held in foreign banks are influenced by differences among countries in interest rates earned on such investments.

In order to react to interest rate differentials, international capital movements must also be relatively free of exchange control or other restrictions. It was, in fact, the removal of such restrictions by most of the European countries in early 1959, and more recently by Japan, that made the balance of payments of the United States much more subject to international financial competition than it had been prior to that time.[19]

The role of interest rate differentials in determining these movements is also stressed by E. M. Bernstein, who observes that "the recorded outflow of U.S. private short-term funds in recent years has been very responsive to interest rates in the United States and abroad" and attributes to the emergence of significant differentials in these rates the "enormous outflow" of U.S. private short-term funds in 1960 and 1961.[20]

Recently, the influence of interest rate differentials on international movements of capital has been called into question on the ground that study of the quarterly data on capital movements during the last several

[19] P. 7. After examining the course of interest rates in the United States, Canada and the United Kingdom, the *Survey* (p. 10) further observed: "The apparent advantage of holding liquid funds abroad based upon interest rate differentials with or without forward cover paralleled the movement of short-term U.S. capital as shown in the available statistics, and a similar movement of other funds as is suggested by the swing from the usual net receipts to net payments on unrecorded transactions."

[20] "Interest Rates and the U.S. Balance of Payments," *Public Policy*, Cambridge, Mass., 1961, pp. 169-187. Subsequently, in a paper presented at the meeting of the American Finance Association on December 28, 1962, Bernstein qualified his position on this point, stressing the importance of other factors in addition to interest rate differentials in causing international capital flows.

years shows little or no significant relation to changes in interest rates.[21] It would, however, be most surprising if a systematic relationship between these variables were to emerge, given the numerous other factors which have influenced international capital flows.[22] But this does not mean that—in any given period and with developments as they actually were except in regard to interest rates—a narrower margin between interest rate levels in the United States and abroad would not have meant a smaller net outflow of liquid funds from this country. Nor can one overlook the possibility that large capital flows motivated by differences in interest yields may, through their effect on the reported balance-of-payments deficit and gold flows, disturb confidence and thereby spark other flows out of any relation to such changes in interest rates as may have occurred in the meantime.

Given the fact that some of the important influences affecting capital movements are not susceptible of measurement, it is not yet clear that statistical analysis can either prove or disprove the traditional view that interest rates are important in their effects on international capital flows. It would also be difficult to conclude from the available data anything as to the extent of the relative change in interest rates that might be needed to produce desired results. It could be that a

---

[21] See paper by Philip W. Bell, "Private Capital Movements and the U.S. Balance-of-Payments Position," in *Factors Affecting the United States Balance of Payments* (Joint Economic Committee), Washington, December 1962, pp. 395-481. Bell's treatment of this question is based on a correlation analysis covering quarterly changes in various types of capital movements since the beginning of 1957. For a defense of the view that "interest rate changes in our money and loan markets relative to those in major foreign financial centers have a marked and prompt effect on capital flows from and to the United States," see the statement by Fred H. Klopstock, Manager, Research Department, Federal Reserve Bank of New York, before the subcommittee on International Exchange and Payments of the Joint Economic Committee on December 13, 1962. A qualitative evaluation of the responsiveness of different types of capital flows to relative degrees of credit availability among countries and relative levels of market interest rates will be found in Stephen H. Axilrod and Ralph A. Young, "Interest Rates and Monetary Policy," *Federal Reserve Bulletin*, September 1962, pp. 1110-1137.

[22] These include, starting with 1957, the balance-of-payments difficulties of the United Kingdom in that year and of several other countries in 1958, the steps toward convertibility of leading foreign currencies at the beginning of 1959, strong speculative pressures on the dollar and on the price of gold in the second half of 1960, the appreciation of the German mark and the Dutch guilder in March 1961, the ensuing speculative movements of the next several months directed largely against the pound, changes in the Canadian tax law at the end of 1960 providing inducements to U.S. companies with Canadian subsidiaries to shift liquid funds to Canada, and the depreciation and stabilization of the Canadian dollar in early 1962.

relatively small change for the United States would be as effective as a much greater change in the case of, say, the United Kingdom.

The role of interest rate differentials in determining the movement of short-term funds may therefore be obscured at times by other influences. In its *Annual Report* for 1961, however, the Board of Governors of the Federal Reserve System makes clear enough its view that a change in short-term interest rates on the downside, with a widening of the differential between domestic and foreign money markets, "could have led to greater outflows of short-term capital and so worsened the balance of payments."[23] The report is less explicit as to whether a change on the upside would have appreciably reduced the very large outflows which did occur or would have been outweighed by other factors. One may detect a certain difference in emphasis between the effects of a reduction and the effects of an increase in interest rates, possibly reflecting the Board's concern that "To reduce these outflows significantly would have required greater restraint on the availability of bank credit and expansion of liquidity than was appropriate for the domestic economy in 1961."[24] This is, no doubt, the more difficult part of the problem—that is, whether and to what degree credit conditions can be tightened, if needed to curtail the outflow of capital, without running counter to domestic objectives and political forces. The new constraints to which the monetary authorities are subject in this regard and some of the implications for broadening the instruments of economic policy are discussed in Chapter IV of this paper.

Responsiveness of Other Capital to Monetary Policy

In considering the sensitivity of long-term capital movements to monetary policy, we need not, for reasons already noted, be concerned by the fact that these categories do not necessarily mean what they appear to: the essential question is whether the items, regardless of what they are called, are amenable to the tools of monetary policy. Walter Gardner[25] has, in fact, made a proposal, advocated also by Robert Triffin[26] with some amendments, for bringing together in one

[23] Board of Governors of the Federal Reserve System, *Annual Report*, 1961, p. 6.

[24] *Ibid.*, p. 32.

[25] *IMF Staff Papers*, May 1961, pp. 195-211.

[26] "The Presentation of U.S. Balance of Payments Statistics, General Comments," in American Statistical Association, *1961 Proceedings of the Business and Economics Statistics Section,* Washington, 1962, pp. 51-57.

TABLE A-2

U.S. BALANCE OF PAYMENTS—GARDNER PRESENTATION
(in billions of U.S. dollars)

					1960 First Half	1960 Second Half[a]
	1957	1958	1959	1960[a]	First Half	Second Half[a]
A. Market Goods and Services						
1. Exports	19.4	16.3	16.2	19.4	9.6	9.8
2. Imports	—13.3	—13.0	—15.3	—14.7	—7.7	—7.0
3. Trade Surplus	6.1	3.3	0.9	4.7	1.9	2.8
4. Net Services (excl. item C)	2.5	1.9	1.6	1.7	0.8	0.9
Total item A	8.6	5.2	2.5	6.4	2.7	3.7
B. Direct Investment	— 2.1	— 1.1	— 1.3	— 1.6	—0.6	—1.0
C. Noncommercial Transaction (excl. item G)						
1. Military expenditures	— 3.2	— 3.4	— 3.0	— 3.0	—1.5	—1.5
2. Government aid abroad	— 2.2[b]	— 2.6	— 2.4	— 2.8	—1.4	—1.4
3. Government interest receipts, etc.	0.3[b]	0.3	0.2	0.3	0.1	0.2
4. Private transfers	— 0.5	— 0.5	— 0.6	— 0.6	—0.3	—0.3
Total item C	— 5.6	— 6.2	— 5.8	— 6.1	—3.1	—3.0
D. Basic Balance (A through C)	0.9	— 2.1	— 4.6	— 1.3	—1.0	—0.3
E. Open-Market Capital (excl. item G)						
1. Portfolio securities, etc.	— 0.5	— 1.4	— 0.4	— 0.4	—0.1	—0.3
2. Short-term						
(a) Assets	— 0.3	— 0.3	— 0.1	— 1.2	—0.2	—1.0
(b) Liabilities to						
(i) Commercial banks	0.1	c	1.4	0.1	0.8	—0.7
(ii) Other	0.6	0.4	0.2	c	—0.1	0.1
3. Net errors	0.8	0.4	0.8	— 0.9	—0.2	—0.7
Total item E	0.7	— 0.9	1.9	— 2.4	0.2	—2.6
F. Exchange-Market Balance (D + E)	1.6	— 3.0	— 2.7	— 3.7	—0.8	—2.9
G. Compensatory Financing						
1. U.S. loans	— 0.4[b]	0	0.4	0	0	0
2. IMF dollar assets	— 0.4	c	0.3	0.7	0.2	0.5
3. Other official dollar assets	c	0.7	0.9	1.8	0.5	0.8
4. Gold	— 0.8	2.3	1.1	1.7	0.1	1.6
Total item G	— 1.6	3.0	2.7	3.7	0.8	2.9
For comparison with Item G above						
Department of Commerce balancing item	— 0.5	3.5	3.8	3.8	1.4	2.4

NOTE: Reproduced from Walter R. Gardner, "An Exchange-Market Analysis of the U.S. Balance of Payments," *IMF Staff Papers*, May 1961, Table 2, p. 206.

[a] Preliminary figures.

[b] Under the Anglo-American Financial Agreement as amended, the United Kingdom borrowed $122 million in 1957 (item G1), paid $73 million of interest (item C3), and repaid $49 million of principal (item C2). These amounts are not entered in the U.S. balance of payments statistics.

[c] Less than $50 million.

Ways of Presenting the Balance of Payments

TABLE A-3

U.S. BALANCE OF PAYMENTS—TRIFFIN PRESENTATION
(years or yearly rates, in billions of dollars)

Line			1950-57	1958	1959	1960
1.	I.	*Gross Current Account Surplus*	6.8	7.2	4.5	7.9
2.		A. Conventional current account	2.2	1.6	—0.6	3.1
3.		B. Military exports under grants	2.2	3.4	3.1	3.0
4.		C. *Plus* military expenditures	2.4	2.3	2.0	1.8
5.	II.	*U.S. Military Programs and Basic Capital Exports*	8.2	9.4	8.4	9.2
6.		A. U.S. Government	7.2	8.3	7.1	7.6
7.		1. Military programs	4.7	5.7	5.1	4.8
8.		a. Export financing	2.2	3.4	3.1	1.8
9.		b. Dollar settlements	2.4	2.3	2.0	3.0
10.		2. Economic programs:	2.5	2.6	2.0	2.8
11.		a. Export financing				2.2
12.		b. Dollar settlements				0.6
13.		B. Direct investment (net)	1.0	1.1	1.3	1.7
14.		1. U.S. capital	1.0	1.1	1.4	1.7
15.		2. Foreign capital (—)	a	a	—0.1	—
16.	III.	*Basic Balance*: I-II	—1.4	—2.1	—3.9	—1.3
17.	IV.	*Open Market Capital*	—0.4	1.2	—1.5	2.7
18.		A. U.S. capital	0.6	1.8	1.0	2.2
19.		B. Foreign capital	—0.6	—0.2	—1.9	—0.2
20.		1. Dollar holdings	—0.4	—0.2	—1.5	—
21.		2. Other	—0.2	—	—0.4	—0.2
22.		C. Errors and omissions	—0.4	—0.4	—0.5	0.6
23.	V.	*Official Settlements*: III-IV	—0.9	—3.3	—2.4	—4.0
24.		A. U.S. gold and convertible currency holdings	—0.2	—2.3	—1.1	—1.7
25.		B. International institutions:	—	—0.3	—0.4	—1.0
26.		1. IMF capital subscription	—	—	1.4	—
27.		2. Dollar holdings (—)	—	—0.3	—1.8	—1.0
28.		C. Foreign monetary authorities' dollar holdings (—)	—0.7	—0.7	—0.9	—1.2

NOTE: Reproduced from Robert Triffin, "The Presentation of U.S. Balance of Payments Statistics, General Comments," in American Statistical Association, *1961 Proceedings of the Business and Economic Statistics Section,* Washington, 1962, Table I, p. 56.

a Unavailable separately, and included with long-term foreign capital (line 21).

SOURCE: *Survey of Current Business.*

group all private capital transactions, both short-term and long-term, excluding only direct investment. This group, designated "open market capital," would be intermediate between transactions comprising a "basic balance" (differing from those here called "basic transactions" by the exclusion of the long-term capital items listed in the intermediate group) and a set of balancing items termed "compensatory financing" by Gardner and "official settlements" by Triffin. Their groups differ from each other, however, not only in terminology and type of detail but also in content because of Gardner's aim to identify and include in his final category certain loans and repayments as "compensatory" when made for balance-of-payments purposes. The presentations developed by Gardner and Triffin to illustrate their proposals are reproduced here as Tables A-2 and A-3, but their original articles and explanatory notes should be consulted for a fuller statement of their views.

Gardner and Triffin seem to place special emphasis on the "volatility"[27] of the items grouped under "open market capital"—a much looser organizing concept, it would appear, than that of sensitivity to monetary policy, and one of less operational significance. Such a broader grouping may nevertheless be consistent with the sensitivity criterion, if further study and experience show that the long-term capital items involved are relatively responsive to monetary conditions and policies. One may doubt that the relation is very strong in the case of transactions in equities, which bulk large in the category of "long-term" capital flows, but it may hold with respect to new bond flotations and other transactions in fixed-interest securities as well as long-term bank credits. If so, there could be considerable merit in a proposal like Gardner's and Triffin's for grouping the latter types of transactions, along with private short-term capital movements, in a category intermediate between "basic transactions" and "official settlements."

"Compensatory Financing" and "Major Special Transactions"

Gardner's endeavor to mold the balancing items ("below the line") according to the concept of compensatory financing merits further comment because of the special interest it offers as an extension of earlier experimental work along this line by the International Monetary

---

[27] Gardner refers to the items included in this group as "all those forms of capital movement that can easily shift from market to market—a sort of footloose capital."

158

Fund[28] and as an application of the distinction which has figured prominently in theoretical discussions between "autonomous" or "spontaneous" capital movements, on the one hand, and "accommodating" or "induced" finance, on the other.[29] Referring first to his twofold grouping above the line ("basic balance" and "open-market capital"), Gardner explains his objectives as follows:

". . . . If this great aggregate of what might be termed autonomous transactions does not balance out, the exchange rate of the country will be pushed up or down, and the authorities must supply whatever compensatory financing is required to keep the rate from moving outside the support points. Thus we have autonomous transactions above the line matched by compensatory financing below the line. The compensatory financing may take the form of a movement of reserves, or a drawing on the International Monetary Fund, or the use of ad hoc loans or other financing for the purpose. It is only as we draw a line of this sort and group above it the autonomous transactions, and group below it the compensatory financing that comes into play only because the autonomous transactions fail to balance, that we see what it is that is pushing the country's international exchange rate up or down and creating an exchange-market problem.[30]

The application of these principles may involve a considerable element of subjective judgment, since the identification of special compensatory financing implies an opinion about the underlying causes and motivations of particular operations. If, for instance, the International Monetary Fund, the International Bank, and various national credit agencies and commercial banks join together in the extension of credits and loans to a particular underdeveloped country, how much of the total amount provided is to be regarded as "compensatory" and how much as "developmental" financing?

Such problems are thoroughly familiar to the proponents of the concept of compensatory financing and do not necessarily invalidate its use as an analytical device.[31] One may wonder, however, if the objectives which it is intended to serve may not be met equally well by the Commerce Department's practice of showing in its summary

[28] This approach was discussed in considerable detail in a section on "The Concept of Compensatory Official Financing" in International Monetary Fund, *Balance of Payments Yearbook, 1938, 1946, 1947,* Washington, 1949, pp. 4-24.

[29] Cf. J. E. Meade, *The Balance of Payments,* Oxford University Press, 1952, p. 11.

[30] *IMF Staff Papers,* May 1961, p. 196.

[31] See, for example, the discussion of "extraordinary financing" in Poul Høst-Madsen, "Measurements of Imbalance in World Payments 1947-58," *IMF Staff Papers,* November 1962, pp. 343-368.

balance-of-payments table a final balance adjusted for "major special transactions" (Table A-4). The emphasis in this case is on the "non-repetitive" nature of transactions having "a major effect on quarterly changes in net payments or receipts, such as subscriptions to international institutions, advance debt repayments or major private transactions." The notion of "major special transactions" is much broader and perhaps more arbitrary in application than that of compensatory financing, but these limitations are made clear in the way in which the data are presented and discussed.

One problem concerning the Commerce Department's practice in this regard is that what is "major" and "special" in the *quarterly* figures may be much less so in the annual data. Thus, one may wish to show a balance for the fourth quarter of 1960 adjusted to exclude such large lumps as the $370 million Ford transaction in the United Kingdom and the $74 million subscription to the International Development Association, but it is much more doubtful that the balance for the whole of the year should be so adjusted.[32]

[32] The special adjustments employed in some of the tables and charts in the present paper (noted in each instance) are limited to the exclusion of extraordinary receipts in the form of unscheduled debt payments to the U.S. Government. In addition all tables and charts exclude the payments of U.S. subscriptions to the International Monetary Fund in 1947 and 1959 (see Table B-1, note a), but these transactions are already omitted from the Commerce Department's summary presentations of the balance of payments (i.e., Table 1 in the regular quarterly balance-of-payments article in the *Survey of Current Business*).

TABLE A-4

PAYMENTS (—) AND RECEIPTS TREATED AS "SPECIAL TRANSACTIONS"
IN THE U.S. BALANCE OF PAYMENTS, 1959-1962

(millions of dollars)

Year and Quarter	Quarterly or Annual Total (millions of dollars)	Detail	Remarks[a]
1959 I	150		Prepayment by Germany of amortization scheduled for 1961-1965 on settlement (original amount $1 billion) which Germany agreed to pay for postwar economic assistance.
II	—100		Special relatively large direct investment transaction in Canada.
IV	285		Prepayment of debt by foreign governments.
1959 Total	335		
1960 II	— 80		Capital contribution by the U.S. to the Inter-American Development Bank.
IV	—444	—370	Payment by a U.S. corporation to purchase minority interests in one of its European subsidiaries.
		— 74	Capital subscription to the International Development Association.
1960 Total	—524		
1961 II	724	649	Extraordinary debt repayments by foreign governments ($587 million by Germany, $40 million by the Netherlands, and $20 millions by the Philippines).
III	— 75	75 }	Receipt of principal and interest advanced from third to second quarter.
IV	—520	40	Prepayment of debt by Italy.
		—150	Private bank loans to Japan, guaranteed in part by U.S. Government.
		—100	Loan to the Philippines subsequent to revaluation of the Philippine currency and reduction in foreign exchange restrictions.
		— 38[b]	Relatively large sales of stock by a foreign company newly registered on a U.S. stock exchange.
		— 62	Capital subscription to the International Development Association.
		—110	Capital subscription to the Inter-American Development Association.
		—100	Very short-term (year-end) deposits with European banks.
1961 Total	129		

(continued)

TABLE A-4 (concluded)

Year and Quarter	Quarterly or Annual Total (millions of dollars)	Detail	Remarks[a]
1962 I	100		Reversal of operation noted in last item listed above (1961 IV).
II	76	60	Payment by France deferred from 1957.
		16	Prepayment of debt by Sweden.
III	471	293	Prepayment of debt by France.
		178	Prepayment of debt by Italy.

[a] The explanations given are derived from the text and tables of the quarterly balance-of-payments articles in the *Survey of Current Business*.

[b] Amount (not specified in source) obtained by difference between detail specified for other items and the total given for the quarter.

SOURCE: U.S. Department of Commerce, *Survey of Current Business*, various issues, 1959-1962.

APPENDIX B

U.S. Balance-of-Payments Statistics

Introductory Note

The balance-of-payments data through 1961 used in the present study and given in Tables B-1 and B-2 are derived from revised estimates prepared by the Balance of Payments Division of the U.S. Department of Commerce and soon to be issued in a new edition of the historical series last published in 1958.[1] Data for 1962 are from the *Survey of Current Business*, September 1962, supplemented by revised estimates for the second quarter and preliminary estimates for the third quarter supplied directly by the Department of Commerce.[2]

In general, the tables given here correspond to the level of detail shown in the summary (seasonally adjusted) table which regularly accompanies the quarterly balance-of-payments article in the *Survey of Current Business*. The presentation and some of the details differ, however, from the *Survey* table in order to permit the compilation of the balance on "basic transactions" which underlies much of the present analysis.

---

[1] U.S. Department of Commerce, *Balance of Payments-Statistical Supplement*, 1958.

[2] The revised estimates for the second quarter and the preliminary estimates for the third quarter of 1962 in Table B-2 correspond to those published in the *Survey of Current Business* for December 1962 (p. 9). The estimates for the first quarter of 1962 in Table B-2 differ, however, very slightly from those in the December 1962 *Survey* because of revisions which become available too late for incorporation in the present study. For the same reason, there are minor discrepancies between some of the figures for January-September 1962 in other tables in this volume compared with the figures that can be obtained by aggregating the quarterly data in the December 1962 *Survey*.

TABLE B-1

U.S. BALANCE OF PAYMENTS, ANNUALLY, 1946-1961
(millions of dollars)

Line	Item	1946	1947	1948	1949	1950
	I. *As Grouped by Commerce Department*					
1.	*U.S. payments, recorded*	13,413	16,325	17,233	16,739	17,751
2.	Merchandise imports	5,073	5,979	7,563	6,879	9,108
3.	Military expenditures	493	455	799	621	576
4.	Other services	1,425	1,774	1,987	2,202	2,344
5.	Remittances and pensions	625	715	617	630	523
6.	Government grants and capital outflows	5,384	6,415a	5,361	5,854	3,935
	U.S. private capital:					
7.	Direct investments	230	749	721	660	621
8.	Long-term portfolio	— 127	49	69	80	495
9.	Short-term	310	189	116	—187	149
10.	*U.S. receipts, recorded*	14,474	16,159	17,059	16,139	14,192
11.	Merchandise exports	11,707	16,015	13,193	12,149	10,117
12.	Military sales	b	b	b	b	b
13.	Investment income	772	1,102	1,340	1,395	1,593
14.	Misc. services	2,256	2,620	2,256	2,307	2,097
15.	Repayments on U.S. government loans	86	294	443	205	295
16.	Foreign long-term investments in U.S.	— 347	— 98	— 172	119	68
17.	Foreign commercial credits to U.S.	0	23	— 1	— 36	22
18.	Unrecorded transactions	195	936	1,179	775	— 21
19.	*Balance on above items*	1,261	4,567	1,005	175	—3,580
20.	*Other transactions, net*	—1,261	—4,567	—1,005	—175	3,580
21.	U.S. gold sales or purchases (—)	— 623	—2,850a	—1,530	—164	1,743
	Increase or decrease (—) in foreign liquid claims on U.S.:					
22.	Monetary authorities ⎱	— 638	—1,717a	525	— 11	1,569
23.	Others ⎰					268
	II. *"Basic Transactions"*					
24.	U.S. payments (2 to 8)	13,103	16,136	17,117	16,926	17,602
25.	U.S. receipts (11 to 16)	14,474	19,933	17,060	16,175	14,170
26.	Balance	1,371	3,797	— 57	—751	—3,432

(continued)

164

Line	Item	1951	1952	1953	1954	1955
	I. *As Grouped by Commerce Department*					
1.	*U.S. payments, recorded*	20,074	20,280	20,103	20,229	22,262
2.	Merchandise imports	11,202	10,838	10,990	10,354	11,527
3.	Military expenditures	1,270	2,054	2,615	2,642	2,901
4.	Other services	2,601	2,874	2,956	2,935	3,367
5.	Remittances and pensions	457	545	617	615	585
6.	Government grants and capital outflows	3,496	2,809	2,542	2,061	2,627
	U.S. private capital:					
7.	Direct investments	508	852	735	667	823
8.	Long-term portfolio	437	214	— 185	320	241
9.	Short-term	103	94	— 167	635	191
10.	*U.S. receipts, recorded*	19,292	18,633	17,612	18,506	20,614
11.	Merchandise exports	14,123	13,319	12,281	12,799	14,280
12.	Military sales	b	b	192	182	200
13.	Investment income	1,882	1,828	1,910	2,227	2,444
14.	Misc. services	2,739	2,845	2,564	2,551	2,880
15.	Repayments on U.S. government loans	305	429	487	507	416
16.	Foreign long-term investments in U.S.	205	166	228	274	390
17.	Foreign commercial credits to U.S.	38	46	— 50	— 34	4
18.	Unrecorded transactions	477	601	339	173	503
19.	*Balance on above items*	—305	—1,046	—2,152	—1,550	—1,145
20.	*Other transactions, net*	305	1,046	2,152	1,550	1,145
21.	U.S. gold sales or purchases (—)	— 53	— 379	1,161	298	41
	Increase or decrease (—) in foreign liquid claims on U.S.:					
22.	Monetary authorities	—485	1,201	943	1,225	700
23.	Others	843	224	48	27	404
	II. *"Basic Transactions"*					
24.	U.S. payments (2 to 8)	19,971	20,186	20,270	19,594	22,071
25.	U.S. receipts (11 to 16)	19,254	18,587	17,662	18,540	20,610
26.	Balance	—717	—1,599	—2,608	—1,054	—1,461

(continued)

165

Line	Item	1956	1957	1958	1959	1960	1961
	I. As Grouped by Commerce Department						
1.	*U.S. payments, recorded*	26,205	28,264	27,650	29,548	31,317	31,805
2.	Merchandise imports	12,804	13,291	12,952	15,310	14,723	14,514
3.	Military expenditures	2,949	3,216	3,435	3,107	3,048	2,947
4.	Other services	3,875	4,245	4,474	4,925	5,417	5,462
5.	Remittances and pensions	665	702	722	791	842	878
6.	Government grants and capital outflows	2,841	3,233	3,131	3,040[a]	3,405	4,051
	U.S. private capital:						
7.	Direct investments	1,951	2,442	1,181	1,372	1,694	1,475
8.	Long-term portfolio	603	859	1,444	926	850	1,006
9.	Short-term	517	276	311	77	1,338	1,472
10.	*U.S. receipts, recorded*	24,727	27,627	23,633	25,393	27,984	29,946
11.	Merchandise exports	17,379	19,390	16,264	16,282	19,459	19,915
12.	Military sales	161	375	300	302	335	406
13.	Investment income	2,662	2,817	2,845	3,043	3,222	3,682
14.	Misc. services	3,393	3,899	3,658	3,849	3,997	4,063
15.	Repayments on U.S. government loans	479	659	544	1,054[c]	636	1,274[c]
16.	Foreign long-term investments in U.S.	593	399	73	709	430	466
17.	Foreign commercial credits to U.S.	60	88	— 51	154	— 95	140
18.	Unrecorded transactions	543	1,157	488	412	— 592	— 602
19.	*Balance on above items*	— 935	520	—3,529	—3,743	—3,925	—2,461
20.	*Other transactions, net*	935	—520	3,529	3,743	3,925	2,461
21.	U.S. gold sales or purchases (—)[d]	— 306	—798	2,275	731[a]	1,702	742
	Increase or decrease (—) in foreign liquid claims on U.S.:						
22.	Monetary authorities	567	—347	752	1,552[a]	1,862	517
23.	Others	674	625	502	1,460	361	1,202
	II. "Basic Transactions"						
24.	U.S. payments (2 to 8)	25,688	27,988	27,339	29,471	29,979	30,333
25.	U.S. receipts (11 to 16)	24,667	27,539	23,684	25,239	28,079	29,806
26.	Balance	—1,021	—449	—3,655	—4,232	—1,900	— 527

ᵃ Data exclude payments of U.S. subscription to the International Monetary Fund as follows: 1947, $2,750 million (of which $687.5 million was paid in gold and $2,062.5 million in noninterest-bearing demand securities); 1959, $1,375 million (of which $344 million was paid in gold and $1,031 million in noninterest-bearing demand securities).

ᵇ Military sales are included in merchandise exports (line 11) and miscellaneous services (line 14) prior to 1953.

ᶜ For unscheduled debt repayments to the U.S. Government, see Table A-4.

ᵈ Includes (starting March 1961) changes in convertible currency holdings of the U.S. monetary authorities.

SOURCE: U.S. Department of Commerce. See introductory note to Appendix B.

TABLE B-2

U.S. Balance of Payments, Quarterly, 1959-1962
(millions of dollars)

Line	Item	1959 I	II	III	IV
	I. *As Grouped by Commerce Department*	SEASONALLY ADJUSTED			
1.	*U.S. payments, recorded*	7,020	7,417	7,570	7,541
2.	Merchandise imports	3,606	3,866	3,976	3,862
3.	Military expenditures	780	797	776	754
4.	Other services	1,167	1,119	1,259	1,300
5.	Remittances and pensions	188	189	218	196
6.	Government grants and capital outflows	802	718a	779	741
	U.S. private capital:				
7.	Direct investments	308	378	322	364
8.	Long-term portfolio	279	199	246	202
9.	Short-term	— 110	71	— 6	122
10.	*U.S. receipts, recorded*	6,068	6,126	6,484	6,715
11.	Merchandise exports	3,864	3,926	4,297	4,195
12.	Military sales	76	83	67	76
13.	Investment income	730	713	755	845
14.	Misc. services	937	946	986	980
15.	Repayments on U.S. government loans	307c	158	159	430c
16.	Foreign long-term investments in U.S.	110	233	203	163
17.	Foreign commercial credits to U.S.	44	67	17	26
18.	Unrecorded transactions	1	229	— 105	287
19.	*Balance on above items*	— 951	—1,062	—1,191	—539
		NOT SEASONALLY ADJUSTED			
20.	*Other transactions, net*	836	1,177	1,259	471
21.	U.S. gold sales or purchases (—)	95	397a	167	72
	Increase or decrease (—) in foreign liquid claims on U.S.:				
22.	Monetary authorities	290	396a	754	256
23.	Others	451	384	338	143
	II. *"Basic Transactions"*	SEASONALLY ADJUSTED			
24.	U.S. payments (2 to 8)	7,130	7,346	7,576	7,419
25.	U.S. receipts (11 to 16)	6,024	6,059	6,467	6,689
26.	Balance	—1,106	—1,287	—1,109	—730

(continued)

Line	Item	1960			
		I	II	III	IV
	I. *As Grouped by Commerce Department*	SEASONALLY ADJUSTED			
1.	*U.S. payments, recorded*	7,549	7,690	8,000	8,078
2.	Merchandise imports	3,801	3,836	3,664	3,422
3.	Military expenditures	771	758	797	722
4.	Other services	1,347	1,375	1,368	1,327
5.	Remittances and pensions	204	205	211	222
6.	Government grants and capital outflows	768	833	826	978
	U.S. private capital:				
7.	Direct investments	324	271	415	684
8.	Long-term portfolio	236	209	170	235
9.	Short-term	98	203	549	488
10.	*U.S. receipts, recorded*	6,865	7,055	7,002	7,062
11.	Merchandise exports	4,657	4,876	4,940	4,986
12.	Military sales	58	122	70	85
13.	Investment income	796	799	765	862
14.	Misc. services	973	988	1,008	1,028
15.	Repayments on U.S. government loans	170	147	172	147
16.	Foreign long-term investments in U.S.	216	180	53	— 19
17.	Foreign commercial credits to U.S.	— 5	— 57	— 6	— 27
18.	Unrecorded transactions	4	—140	— 159	— 297
19.	*Balance on above items*	—680	—775	—1,157	—1,313
		NOT SEASONALLY ADJUSTED			
20.	*Other transactions, net*	641	891	1,191	1,202
21.	U.S. gold sales or purchases (—)	50	94	637	921
	Increase or decrease (—) in foreign liquid claims on U.S.:				
22.	Monetary authorities	153	462	596	651
23.	Others	438	335	— 42	— 370
	II. *"Basic Transactions"*	SEASONALLY ADJUSTED			
24.	U.S. payments (2 to 8)	7,451	7,487	7,451	7,590
25.	U.S. receipts (11 to 16)	6,870	7,112	7,008	7,089
26.	Balance	—581	—375	— 443	— 501

(continued)

Line	Item	1961			
		I	II	III	IV
	I. *As Grouped by Commerce Department*	SEASONALLY ADJUSTED			
1.	U.S. payments, recorded	7,690	7,411	8,082	8,622
2.	Merchandise imports	3,369	3,417	3,840	3,888
3.	Military expenditures	770	756	699	722
4.	Other services	1,309	1,337	1,388	1,428
5.	Remittances and pensions	221	221	216	220
6.	Government grants and capital outflows	962	804	1,094	1,191
	U.S. private capital:				
7.	Direct investments	457	269	429	320
8.	Long-term portfolio	120	218	194	474
9.	Short-term	482	389	222	379
10.	U.S. receipts, recorded	7,400	7,953	6,979	7,614
11.	Merchandise exports	5,061	4,768	4,940	5,146
12.	Military sales	71	150	88	97
13.	Investment income	941	888	866	987
14.	Misc. services	996	1,022	997	1,048
15.	Repayments on U.S. government loans	133	851c	81	209c
16.	Foreign long-term investments in U.S.	122	201	20	123
17.	Foreign commercial credits to U.S.	76	73	— 13	4
18.	Unrecorded transactions	— 29	—366	193	— 400
19.	Balance on above items	—319	176	—910	—1,408
		NOT SEASONALLY ADJUSTED			
20.	Other transactions, net	308	— 89	909	1,333
21.	U.S. gold sales or purchases (—)d	346	—330	270	456
	Increase or decrease (—) in foreign liquid claims on U.S.:				
22.	Monetary authorities	36	—329	405	405
23.	Others	— 74	570	234	472
	II. *"Basic Transactions"*	SEASONALLY ADJUSTED			
24.	U.S. payments (2 to 8)	7,208	7,022	7,860	8,243
25.	U.S. receipts (11 to 16)	7,324	7,880	6,992	7,610
26.	Balance	116	858	—868	— 633

(continued)

170

Line	Item	1962		
		I	II	IIIᵖ
	I. *As Grouped by Commerce Department*	SEASONALLY ADJUSTED		
1.	*U.S. payments, recorded*	8,291	8,093	8,282
2.	Merchandise imports	3,920	4,032	4,130
3.	Military expenditures	752	746	730
4.	Other services	1,388	1,450	1,473
5.	Remittances and pensions	234	223	221
6.	Government grants and capital outflows	1,050	1,059	1,118
	U.S. private capital:			
7.	Direct investments	229	400	300
8.	Long-term portfolio	398	284	137
9.	Short-term	320	—101	173
10.	*U.S. receipts, recorded*	7,709	8,001	8,057
11.	Merchandise exports	5,070	5,339	5,170
12.	Military sales	220ᵇ	241ᵇ	226ᵇ
13.	Investment income	1,026	1,052	948
14.	Misc. services	1,067	1,121	1,084
15.	Repayments on U.S. government loans	160	220ᶜ	616ᶜ
16.	Foreign long-term investments in U.S.	160	111	13
17.	Foreign commercial credits to U.S.	6	— 83	0
18.	Unrecorded transactions	106	—134	—494
19.	*Balance on above items*	—476	—226	—719
		NOT SEASONALLY ADJUSTED		
20.	*Other transactions, net*	462	312	738
21.	U.S. gold sales or purchases (—)ᵈ	190	—207	550
	Increase or decrease (—) in foreign liquid claims on U.S.:			
22.	Monetary authorities	—420	529	625
23.	Others	692	— 10	—437
	II. *"Basic Transactions"*	SEASONALLY ADJUSTED		
24.	U.S. payments (2 to 8)	7,971	8,194	8,109
25.	U.S. receipts (11 to 16)	7,703	8,084	8,057
26.	Balance	—268	—110	— 52

NOTES TO TABLE B-2

ᵃ See note a, Table B-1.

ᵇ Includes $125 million in the first quarter, $88 million in the second quarter, and $58 million in the third quarter of 1962 for amounts transferred to restricted accounts with the U.S. Treasury on military purchases to be made by foreign countries (see *Survey of Current Business*, June 1962, p. 12).

ᶜ For unscheduled debt repayments to the U.S. Government, see Table A-4.

ᵈ Includes (starting March 1961) changes in convertible currency holdings of the U.S. monetary authorities.

ᵖ Preliminary.

SOURCE: U.S. Department of Commerce. See introductory note to Appendix B, including explanation of minor discrepancies between the estimates given here for the first quarter of 1962 and those appearing in the *Survey of Current Business* for December 1962.

172

Index